£1.
U40

Past-into-Present Series

THE NAVY

T K Butcher

B T BATSFORD LTD London

First published 1973
© T. K. Butcher, 1973

To those who served in Coastal Forces 1939–1945

Printed in Great Britain by
Redwood Press Ltd, Trowbridge, Wiltshire
for the publishers
B. T. Batsford Ltd, 4 Fitzhardinge Street, London W1H 0AH
ISBN 0 7134 1794 3

359

Acknowledgments

The Author and Publisher would like to thank the following for the illustrations which appear in the book: the Ashmolean Museum (Sutherland Collection), Oxford for fig. 13; the British Museum for figs 4 and 5; the Central Office of Information (Crown copyright) for figs 55, 62 and 63; the Imperial War Museum for figs 34, 39–41, 43–54, 57–59; the Mansell Collection for figs 36, 60; the Ministry of Defence, Royal Navy (Crown copyright) for figs 42, 61, 64 and 65; the Musée de la Maritime, Paris for fig. 30; the National Maritime Museum for figs 6, 7, 9, 14, 15, 17–20, 22–27, 31 and 32; the National Maritime Museum, Greenwich Hospital Collection for fig. 11; the National Portrait Gallery for figs 12, 16, 28 and 37; the Rijksmuseum, Amsterdam for fig. 10; Russel and Sons Ltd for fig. 29.

They also wish to thank Victor Gollancz Ltd for permission to quote an extract from *Very Ordinary Seaman* by J. P. W. Mallalieu (1944, reissued 1970) and William Heinemann Ltd for the extract from *Three Rows of Tape* by A. Trystan Edwards.

Contents

Acknowledgments		2
List of Illustrations		5
1	The Foundations of the Navy	7
2	The Seventeenth Century: Triumphs and Disaster	19
3	War and Peace in the Eighteenth Century	30
4	The Napoleonic Wars	43
5	Trafalgar to Scapa Flow	58
6	The Second World War	69
7	The Navy in the Nuclear Age	86
Further Reading		92
Index		94

The Illustrations

1	A Viking ship, reconstruction	8
2	Carving of a medieval ship	9
3	Medieval soldiers sail for France	10
4	Henry VIII's ships	11
5	Dover harbour in Tudor times	12
6	The *Ark Royal*	14
7	The Armada	16
8	Sir Francis Drake	18
9	The *Royal Sovereign*	20
10	Sea fight, 1607	21
11	Robert Blake	22
12	Samuel Pepys	24
13	The Dutch attacking Chatham	26
14	The Captain's cabin	31
15	Quiberon Bay	32
16	Admiral Hood	33
17	Naval dockyard	34
18	A purser	35
19	A seaman	36
20	A captain	37
21	The Moonlight Battle	39
22	Press-gang	41
23	Recruiting poster	44
24	The Glorious First of June	46
25	Parker presenting the List of Grievances	47
26	Admiral Duncan	48
27	Battle of the Nile	49
28	Lord Nelson	50
29	Gun deck of HMS *Victory*	52
30	Battle of Trafalgar	53
31	Nelson wounded	54
32	Aboard a warship, 1820	55
33	Flogging	56
34	HMS *Warrior*	57
35	*Punch* cartoon about pay	58
36	The stoke hole	59
37	Admiral Fisher	60
38	Bombardment in the Dardanelles	62
39	Admiral Jellicoe	63
40	Admiral Beatty	65
41	Battle of Jutland	66
42	An early submarine	67
43	*Hindenburg* scuttled	68
44	Battle of the River Plate	70
45	Günther Prien	71
46	Evacuation from Dunkirk	72
47	Italian battleship steaming to surrender	73
48	The *Ark Royal* sinking	74
49	Destroyer in heavy seas	75
50	A Flower class corvette	76
51	Small craft patrol	77
52	Supplies for Malta	79
53	U-boat firing a torpedo	80
54	U-boat being sunk	80
55	Cleaning the guns	81
56	Ship in icy conditions	82
57	Landing ship	83
58	Landing beach, Normandy	84
59	Midget submarine	85
60	The rum ration	87
61	A guided-missile destroyer	88
62	Remote control for engines	89
63	A messdeck	90
64	A training ship	91
65	Nuclear-powered submarine	93

1 The Foundations of the Navy

The professional fighting force we know as the Royal Navy is a comparatively recent development, but our origins as a seafaring race lie far back in our history. Seafarers were among our earliest ancestors, as we find in an Anglo-Saxon poem *The Seafarer* from which this vivid passage describes life at sea in any age:

> Wild were the waves when I took my turn,
> The arduous nightwatch, standing at the prow
> While the boat tossed near the rocks. My feet
> Were tortured by frost, fettered
> In frozen chains; fierce anguish clutched
> At my heart; passionate longing maddened
> The heart of the sea-weary man. Prosperous men
> Living on land do not begin to understand
> How I, careworn and cut off from my kinsmen
> Have as an exile endured the winter
> On the icy sea.
>
> *Translation by Kevin Crossley Holland*

This poem comes down the centuries with an immediate shock of recognition to anyone who has kept a middle watch (midnight to 4 a.m.) in the northern waters!

The Anglo-Saxon seafarer, brave and hardy though he undoubtedly was, was also a cruel and bloodthirsty pirate, raiding defenceless coastal villages and showing no mercy to those he attacked.

The same brutality towards his enemies was shown by another sailor, described centuries later by Geoffrey Chaucer as one of the pilgrims who rode to Canterbury. This 'shipman' was a fourteenth-century skipper from the port of Dartmouth in Devon, and although Chaucer describes him cynically as 'certainly a good fellow', he was not above stealing the Bordeaux wine entrusted to him as cargo. He also had a short way with prisoners: unless they were rich enough to be ransomed, over the side they went.

> If that he fought, and had the higher hand,
> By water he sent them home to every land.

 A reconstruction of a Viking ship

He was a skilled seaman and an expert navigator, who knew every harbour between the Baltic and Cape Finisterre, and even every creek between the coasts of Brittany and Spain.

It was about the time of Chaucer's birth that English ships began to be formed, in times of danger, into a fighting force which was a kind of temporary Navy. In the reign of Edward III British ships won a victory against the French at Sluys. This was a brutal affair, described by the chronicler Froissart as 'very murderous and horrible . . . all the Normans and others were killed or drowned, so that not one of them escaped'.

The Tudor Navy

If we look for the real beginnings of our Navy, we must consider Henry VIII as its founder, for he was the first English King to build ships as a permanent means of defence against his enemies. His first great warship, the *Henry Grace à Dieu*, commonly known after him as the *Great Harry*, was a rather cumbersome vessel of 1,000 tons, with three tiers of guns and carrying 700 men, including soldiers. This, and his other ships, were paid for by the King himself, out of the wealth he had seized from the monasteries, and this Navy was intended to defend him against attack by the supporters of the Pope.

It was during Henry's reign that an idea was introduced which was to revolutionise warfare at sea and to lay the foundations of Britain's maritime power. This was the mounting of heavy guns in ships, said to have been developed by a naval architect named James Baker. Artillery had been much improved on land in the Low Countries, where the new muzzle-loading guns had been effectively

2 Carving of a medieval ship in the church at Tiverton, Devon

used against fortified towns, but these weapons were so heavy that they would capsize a ship if they were mounted on its upper decks. The brilliant and revolutionary idea was to place them on lower gun decks, where they could be fired through portholes called gunports, and their weight thus distributed without danger of capsizing the ship.

Henry's daughter, Queen Elizabeth I, built on the foundations he had laid, and although she was niggardly over supplying the Navy with money, the financial control was in the hands of an extremely competent seaman and businessman, Sir John Hawkins. Hawkins had made his name in the slave trade by kidnapping unfortunate negroes from the West African coast and selling them to the Spanish planters in the West Indies and South America. This inhuman trade had been entirely in the hands of the Spaniards, whose King had strictly forbidden trading with foreigners. Hawkins had considerable success at first, but on his third slaving voyage he lost most of his men and ships, including one vessel belonging to the Queen.

The main object of British seamen was now to challenge the Spaniards for the riches of the New World, the gold and silver which were making Spain the wealthiest country in Europe. Sir Francis Drake and others made voyages to the

Caribbean, known as the Spanish Main, looting and pillaging wherever they went. The Queen supported these expeditions and when Drake suggested the bold plan of sailing through the Straits of Magellan to plunder the Spanish treasure ships in the Pacific, she gave him a ship of her own and a large sum of money. As a final proof of her support, she presented him with a sword, with the words 'He which striketh at thee, Drake, striketh at me'.

One of Drake's ships was lost with all hands shortly after rounding the southern tip of South America; another was broken up, and the Queen's own ship, the *Elizabeth*, turned back. Drake himself, in the *Golden Hind*, sailed on into the Pacific, which the King of Spain regarded as his private ocean. Thus a Spanish treasure ship which they met proved to be unarmed and was easily captured. An anonymous account of the voyage says 'we found in her great riches, as jewels and precious stones, 13 chests full of royals of plate, fourscore pound weight of gold, and 26 ton of silver'.

A Spanish officer who spent several days as a prisoner aboard the *Golden Hind* described how Drake lived. He 'carries with him nine or ten cavaliers, younger sons of noble English houses. He is served on silver dishes with gold borders and gilded garlands, in which are his coat of arms. He carries all possible dainties and perfumed waters, many of them given him by the Queen'. Nobody thought of describing how the ordinary sailors lived aboard the *Golden Hind*, but as we shall see, there were no dainties or perfumed waters for them.

Apart from seizing treasure from the Spaniards, Drake's expedition had another object, to find territory in the New World where an English settlement could be made. His choice was Drake's Bay, near where the city of San Francisco now

3 English soldiers sailing for France in Chaucer's time

4 Henry VIII's ships leaving Dover for the Field of the Cloth of Gold, 1520

stands. The pleasant climate and the friendly attitude of the inhabitants, added to the fact that no Europeans had ever before landed there, made it most attractive. After his return home, Drake asked the Queen if he could be Governor of a colony in what he called 'New Albion', but the project never came to anything.

Drake's return to England, after a voyage round the world lasting three years, found him a national hero, although his arrogance and boasting made him some enemies, especially among those who wanted peace with Spain. In spite of all that had happened, England was not at war with the Spaniards, and King Philip's Ambassador in London protested vigorously about Drake's acts of piracy. Nevertheless, Queen Elizabeth kept a large share of the plunder (the other shareholders made an enormous profit). The *Golden Hind* was brought to London and Drake gave the Queen a splendid banquet, at the end of which she knighted him, in the presence of the Spanish Ambassador.

It was now only a matter of time before the unofficial war between England and Spain became an open war. After his ships defeated the Portuguese in 1582, Philip II became ruler of a vast empire: as well as Spain and Portugal, he was in command of Mexico, Florida, the West Indies, the South American coast, Naples, Sicily, the Azores, the Canary and Cape Verde Islands, the Guinea Coast of West Africa, Angola, Mozambique, Goa, Malacca, Macao and the Philippines.

To provoke a world power like this was audacious to the point of foolhardiness and that was exactly what England continued to do. In 1585 Drake took 25 ships

5 A bird's eye view of Dover harbour in the time of Henry VIII

manned by the country's best seamen and carrying as many soldiers as could be accommodated, on an expedition to the Caribbean. There they plundered the Spanish possessions, attacked and held to ransom their most important cities and sailed home in triumph.

For the King of Spain this was the final insult. He had resisted for a long time the pressure from his High Admiral to make a massive attack on the impudent English in their own island. By the beginning of 1587 the preparations for an invasion were well advanced and England was largely unprepared. Something had to be done, and Sir Francis Drake urged the Queen to give him a free hand 'to smoke the wasps out of their nests'.

The Queen agreed and in April Drake set out from Plymouth on his famous expedition 'to singe the King of Spain's beard'. Under his command were four royal ships, equipped and paid for by the Government, and 22 more provided by the merchants of the City of London, who expected great profits from the plunder brought back.

Drake's ships first attacked Cadiz, Spain's most important naval base, where the Armada, the great fleet intended for the invasion of England, was already being fitted out under the protection of shore batteries. There was also a fleet of galleys, long low ships propelled by oarsmen and with guns trained forward. At the bow and stern were raised decks known as the forecastle and after-castle, crowded with soldiers ready to board an enemy ship as soon as it came alongside.

Drake led his ships in line ahead (that is, each one following behind the other, rather than sailing abreast), relying on their powerful broadside fire power. He crippled two galleys almost immediately, sank a galleon and then put four more galleys out of action. By nightfall he had destroyed a great part of the Spanish fleet, and next morning, when the rest of the galleys attacked, he easily beat them off with tremendous losses in enemy ships and men. Drake's fleet returned to England unscathed, having delayed the sailing of the Armada for a whole year, and with a tremendous store of plunder from Spanish and Portuguese ships. It was now necessary to follow up this victory by keeping command of the seas and preventing the Spaniards from even mounting their proposed invasion. Drake and Lord Howard of Effingham, the Lord Admiral, pressed this view vigorously, but were overruled.

Once again the Spaniards began to prepare their fleet and their army, for the invasion was now to be what we should call a combined operation. The Armada, or sea force, was to sail up the Channel, defeat the English Navy and then cover the soldiers, who were to cross from Belgium in flat-bottomed boats and land in the Thames estuary.

To face them was the English fleet, which included, in a total of nearly 200, only 34 ships of what we can now call the Royal Navy. On the whole the English vessels were better armed than the enemy, who still relied on the old method of sea warfare, going alongside the enemy and boarding with pike and sword. The English were in good heart, cheered by their previous successes: as Lord Howard wrote, 'there is here the gallantest company of captains, soldiers and mariners that I think ever was seen in England'.

Towards the end of May in the year 1588 the Spanish Armada set sail from Lisbon. The weather was against them from the start, and storms in the Bay of Biscay drove them into the harbours of Northern Spain. Drake was, as always, keen to attack the enemy as soon as possible, but the Government was cautious. In the event it was Howard who defied their wishes and sailed southward in an attempt to meet the enemy, but contrary winds forced him to return.

In those days, with ships completely at the mercy of the prevailing winds, it was almost impossible to find out the enemy's movements and the Armada was already in sight of the Lizard before the news reached Plymouth.

The English fleet put to sea in great haste and confronted the Armada just in

6 The *Ark Royal*, English flagship in the fight against the Spanish Armada, 1588

time. With any further delay the Spaniards would have been able to destroy them one by one as they came out of Plymouth Sound. Once again the broadsides of heavy guns from the English ships took speedy toll of the enemy. Before long the Armada had taken a fair battering, although the main body was still intact. Howard decided to follow the enemy up the Channel; after a second action off the Isle of Wight the Spaniards were able to anchor off Calais. Although the second part of their invasion force was not yet ready to embark from Belgium, the Spaniards were still in a strong position. The Armada had to be harried at once, and a method was quickly decided. Eight ships were filled with pitch and resin, set on fire and dispatched towards the enemy. There was immediate confusion among the Spaniards—many ships cut their cables and collided in an attempt to avoid the fireships. The English attacked the straggling fleet and inflicted considerable losses, but owing to lack of ammunition and supplies, they were not able to consolidate their victory by completely destroying the invaders.

That task was undertaken by the weather and the inhospitable coastline of Scotland and Ireland, around which the fleeing Spaniards had to sail to avoid their enemy in the Channel. Many Spanish ships were wrecked during the voyage round the north of Scotland and through the Irish Sea and only 9,000 men from the 'invincible Armada' ever saw their homeland again.

England had now established herself beyond challenge as a great sea power, having defeated the mighty Spaniards' long-planned attempt at invasion. The victory could not have been achieved without the courage and endurance of the ordinary English sailor.

The Elizabethan Seaman

What sort of man was he and how was he treated? Rough and illiterate he certainly was, although to have served with Drake or Hawkins gave him some status if he survived to tell of his exploits in his home town, especially if he brought prize money with him. He could be obstinate and difficult ('stroppy' is the modern naval term), especially with inexperienced officers or those he considered untrustworthy. Sir William Monson, who served against the Armada, wrote: 'The seamen are stubborn or perverse when they perceive their commander is ignorant of the discipline of the sea, and cannot speak to them in their own language'.

The Elizabethan seaman's pay of 10 shillings (50p) a month, although quite good for those days (it had been much less before 1585), was hard-earned. Apart from the danger of being killed, wounded or captured, he had to live under almost unendurable conditions during a long voyage. The *Golden Hind*, though only about 60 feet (18 metres) long and with a width of 18 feet (5 metres), held a complement of over 90 men during her voyage round the world.

The ordinary sailor had only one suit of working clothes to last throughout the longest voyage, and in it he slept on the wooden deck. His clothes would often become soaked and stiff with salt and dirt. It was only when John Hawkins saw the natives in the West Indies sleeping in 'hammacoes' slung from trees that he introduced hammocks into his ships, and their use spread rapidly in the royal ships. They lasted until modern times as a comfortable and easily stowed sleeping place, both at sea and in crowded naval barracks. They have the additional advantage that they can swing when the ship rolls in heavy seas, and thus the sleeper does not roll out, as he might in a bunk.

Food during a long voyage was scarce and often inedible. Salted meat and fish, ship's biscuit and cheese were the mainstays, for they could normally be kept for long periods. If the civilian contractors who supplied the ships were dishonest, as they all too frequently were, the meat was of inferior quality and the contents of the casks were putrid when opened. The drink was often even worse: the daily ration was one gallon of beer, but as it was brewed without hops it soon went sour and caused enteritis, especially in the tropics. Scurvy, caused by lack of fresh fruit and vegetables, was always a scourge during long voyages.

7 The first engagement between the English fleet and the Armada

Medical knowledge was almost non-existent, and disease, prevalent as it was ashore and accepted as an inevitable fact of life, was completely unchecked in crowded and insanitary conditions at sea. Even during the actions against the Armada, the English fleet was ravaged by sickness, and afterwards Lord Howard wrote to Lord Burghley, the Lord Treasurer: 'It would grieve any man's heart to see them that have served so valiantly to die so miserably'. The only attempt to disinfect the ships, by burning broom between decks, had no effect. When put ashore the men were in a pitiable state: Howard's letter continues: 'Sickness and mortality begin wonderfully amongst us: and it is a most pitiful sight to see here at Margate how the men, having no place to receive them into here, die in the streets. I am driven myself, of force, to come ashore, to see them bestowed in some lodgings; and the best I can get is barns and out-houses; and the relief is small that I can provide for them there'. He went on to ask for money from the Navy's funds to supply clothing for his distressed sailors: 'My Lord, I would think it a marvellous good way that there were a thousand pounds worth or two thousand marks worth of hose, doublets, shirts, shoes and suchlike sent down ... for else, in very short time, I look to see most of the mariners go naked'.

If the sailors who fought the Armada were scarcely treated as national heroes during their service, their fate when discharged to go home was little better. If a man were disabled, his own parish was supposed to be responsible for maintaining him, and with luck he might be granted a license to beg for a period of one year.

Several Pension Acts were passed in Queen Elizabeth's reign—the first was in 1593, five years after the Armada. The largest sums awarded were £10 for a sailor and £20 for an officer, but most were considerably less.

As we have seen from his letter to the Lord Treasurer, Howard had a strong feeling of compassion towards his men; this was unfortunately not shared by all his officers. Drake, though usually chivalrous towards his prisoners, could be sadly lacking in attention to the welfare of his own crews. Complaints of 'weak victualling and filthy drink' were common; during Drake's 'beard-singeing' expedition in 1587, they were serious enough to cause a mutiny aboard one of his ships, the *Golden Lion*. Drake sentenced the mutineers to death, but in fact no action was taken against them. Two years later, when Drake again attacked the Spanish coast, he lost nearly half of his 12,000 men from sickness.

Reward and punishment
During Elizabeth's reign we can see the development of the Navy in several ways. The most important was that the Queen's ships, if only as a small minority of the total force, were in action against the enemy. Then towards the end of the Queen's reign there were the beginnings of some kind of naval uniform. When a man's working suit finally wore out, it had to be replaced, and he could either buy a new one from the purser or buy cloth to make himself an outfit. So it came about that approximately similar clothing would be worn by the whole ship's company. We can get an idea of the kind of clothing from a bill of 1595 for the supply of 200 suits, 400 shirts, woollen and worsted stockings, linen breeches and Monmouth caps (similar to a modern tam o'shanter).

As the custom of buying replacements of clothing from the purser became more usual, it was necessary for the seaman to receive some pay in advance, instead of having to wait until the end of the voyage. The real value of money declined sharply during Elizabeth's reign, and unless he was very lucky with prize money, a man was unlikely to bring home enough to support his family for long.

As for prize money, this varied a great deal and the ordinary sailor stood little chance of making his fortune. When the treasure ship *Madre de Dios* was captured off the Azores in 1592, the Queen proposed that each man should get twenty shillings (£1) as his share, her own being a return of £90,000 for her investment of £3,000! On this occasion at least, the sailors took their revenge, and hardly a man went ashore without a handful of diamonds or pearls.

The maintenance of 'good order and naval discipline' in a ship at sea is always important: a thief on the messdeck can thoroughly upset a good crew, and a man who is drunk or asleep on watch endangers the whole ship. Thus it is not surprising to find the beginnings of a system of punishment in Elizabethan ships. A sailor who committed murder on board was tied hand and foot to his victim and thrown overboard, while a gun was fired to draw attention to the crime. A thief was ducked three times from the bowsprit and then put ashore with nothing but a loaf of bread. For being found asleep on watch there were graduated punishments, from being placed at the mainmast with a bucket of water on the head for the first offence, to being 'hanged on the bowsprit end of the ship in a basket, with a can of beer and a loaf of bread and a sharp knife: choose him to hang there till he starve or cut himself into the sea.' This punishment was only carried out after the fourth offence. As for drunkenness on board, this was punishable by confinement in the bilboes (rather like the stocks) for as long as the captain felt it was necessary.

It is probable that punishments were more often needed aboard the Queen's ships, whose crews were usually made up by the press-gang, than in privately owned vessels like Drake's *Golden Hind*. The famous captains never had any lack of volunteers, however dangerous the enterprise, whether it was sailing round the world or crossing the Atlantic to Newfoundland in a tiny ship of 10 tons like Sir Humphrey Gilbert's *Squirrel*.

8 Sir Francis Drake

2 The Seventeenth Century: Triumphs and Disaster

After the death of Queen Elizabeth in 1603, the Navy went through a period of shameful decline. James I did not keep up the hard-won advantage against the Spaniards; instead he pursued a negative policy of peace. He stopped the system of 'letters of marque', which gave privately-owned ships the right to attack and seize enemy vessels (in this case Spanish) without being treated as pirates if captured.

As no other country followed suit, the unfortunate Englishman was practically driven off the seas. Our place as a trading nation was taken by the Dutch; the royal fleet rotted at its moorings and hardly ever put its bows out of harbour. With no chance of employment from his home ports, the English sailor's only hope was to go to Holland and work for his successful rivals.

Charles I

When Charles I became King in 1625, the situation was truly desperate, with piracy unchecked in the Channel and no money to build up the fleet again. His solution was to tax the country to provide 'ship money', but he thought of it at the worst possible time. The King was already beginning his attempt to abolish Parliament and rule the country without it. The English people naturally objected to paying for a fleet which would be controlled by the King rather than by their own representatives, and there were suspicions that the money would be used for other purposes.

The opposition to ship money was led by John Hampden, but when he was brought to trial, he lost his case. The King proved that in this instance the distrust of his people was unfounded, for he actually spent the money on building a small Navy. By the time the Civil War between King and Parliament broke out, some of the royal ships were beginning to clear the Channel of enemy vessels. In a small way, this was another milestone in the history of the Navy, for these ships had, even if under protest, been paid for by the country and not by the King himself.

Unfortunately for Charles I, however, the major part of the 'Ship Money Fleet' took the Parliamentary side, and was strong enough to prevent the European powers from helping him. If the French had been able to intervene on the King's side, the result of the Civil War would almost certainly have been different. Towards the end, the fleet was divided, following strenuous efforts by the Royalists to win it over, but the only result was a stalemate. Prince Rupert, who had already

9 Charles I's Navy: the *Royal Sovereign*, 1637

proved himself a dashing cavalry commander, kept the Royalist part of the fleet at sea under his command for some time after the King's land forces had been defeated.

The Dutch Wars

After the execution of Charles I, Cromwell built up the Navy as part of his policy of making England strong again. As a dictator, he found no difficulty in raising the money by taxes, and there was a plentiful supply of timber from the estates seized from the King's supporters. As soon as his fleet was strong enough, he attacked the Dutch. This small nation had not only won its freedom from Spanish rule, but had followed up its victories on land by taking the Spanish trade at sea. The First Dutch War, as it is usually called, was therefore a trade war, like those which were to follow. After several actions off our own coasts and in the Channel, the English fleet won a decisive victory in 1653 off Scheveningen. The great Dutch admiral Tromp was killed and the war was won. Superior gunnery and the English method of attack in line ahead had triumphed over a skilful enemy. It is pleasant to read that one of the instructions to the fleet laid down that 'if in time of fight God shall deliver any of the enemy's ships into our hands, special care is to be taken to save their men as the present state of our condition will permit in such a case'.

The lot of the ordinary sailor had been very poor indeed in Charles I's fleet. Dishonest contractors were still lining their pockets by supplying inferior food and drink, and short measure at that. Large bribes to members of the Navy Board, responsible for placing the contracts, made it certain that complaints were ignored. On board the ships, the pursers who issued the rations often gave out 14 ounces instead of a pound (56 grams short), and made up their inadequate pay out of the proceeds of their dishonesty.

Conditions for seamen

As far as food was concerned, Parliament treated its seamen no better than the King had done; contractors and pursers had too strong a hold to be broken. However, there were some improvements. Pay was increased to 19 shillings (95p) a month, and promptly paid, though there were deductions for a benevolent fund, for the chaplain and for the surgeon. In case of sickness, a man was better

10 A seventeenth-century sea fight: the destruction of the Spanish flagship at Gibraltar, 1607

treated when put ashore, where he could receive such primitive medical attention as was available in those days.

During the First Dutch War, the London hospitals were ordered to make beds available for wounded seamen, and the same happened in several seaports. A great advance was the Board of Commissions for the Sick and Wounded, set up in 1653. It was given power to make payments of up to £10 for wounded men and to grant pensions of up to £6 13s 4d (£6.67). An allowance of £5 every six months was made to each ship, to provide medical supplies. In the same year of 1653, pay was again raised to 24 shillings (£1.20) a month for able seamen and 19 shillings (95p) for ordinary seamen. The possibility of promotion from seaman to midshipman was opened up by an order that a certain number of men in each ship were to be so promoted. With the rapid expansion of the Navy, prospects for advancement had never been better.

A final improvement at this time was a fair distribution of prize money. In Elizabeth's reign there were no rules and everyone grabbed what he could. In 1649, an Act of Parliament laid down fixed rates. The crew of a ship which destroyed an enemy vessel received half the value of the victim, a value calculated on the number of her guns. The other half was paid into a fund to help the sick, wounded, widows and orphans. In the case of a merchant ship captured as a prize, one third of the value went to the ship's company, including the officers, one third to the relief fund, and the remaining share to the State.

11   Robert Blake

The Navy was much better led during the Commonwealth period than it had been since Elizabethan days. Under James I, the fleet was encumbered by too many courtiers without any training or experience at sea. The results of incompetent leadership could be disastrous; the Duke of Buckingham, who had succeeded Howard as Lord High Admiral, lost 4,000 of his force of 5,500 men during an attack on French ports in 1625.

Charles I's courtiers followed the fashion for a summer voyage as 'fair weather sailors', but the Parliamentary Navy was a much more professional affair. Of its commanders, Robert Blake is the most famous, but Edward Popham, Richard Deane, William Penn, Edward Montagu and George Monk (afterwards Duke of Albemarle) deserve to be mentioned in any history of the Navy. Of these, only Popham and Penn had been trained at sea, all the others having first made their name as army officers. Their title 'general-at-sea' is an indication of the lack of distinction at that time between a military and a naval command. They were followed equally readily by their men, not only for their courage and resource in action, but because they really cared about the welfare of their crews. It was largely due to them that the many improvements already mentioned were carried through.

Problems of pay
The Commonwealth, then, was on the whole a good time for the Navy, with its prestige raised again to something approaching its level in Elizabethan times and with better conditions all round. However, it did not last, and once again peace meant that England's sailors were neglected and forgotten. They had already begun to feel the pinch towards the end of the Cromwellian period, because heavy taxes had drained the country's resources and they were no longer paid regularly. By the time of the Restoration of Charles II in 1660, some seamen were owed as much as three years back pay.

History was repeating itself; with the return of peace, the Navy had been allowed to run down, and the Dutch had once again taken command of the seas and consequently of the trade routes. The new King was in a difficult position, with the country bankrupt and the Navy alone in debt to the sum of £1¼ million.

Charles appointed his brother, James Duke of York, as Lord High Admiral, and fortunately he proved to be the right man for the job. His task was far from easy, because of the enormous debt, coupled with Parliament's reluctance to vote money for the upkeep of the fleet. A good start was made by settling the arrears of the seamen's pay, and for several years their accounts were kept in order.

Then the Navy Board ran out of cash, and the men were paid by 'ticket'. This was a promissory note or 'promise to pay', which could only be cashed at the Pay Office in London. The result was obvious—the average sailor could not afford the

12 Samuel Pepys

journey, so 'ticket touts' in the naval ports offered to cash the notes for one quarter or even one third of their value.

Even if a seaman presented his ticket at the Pay Office, there was often no money to pay him. Samuel Pepys, who became Secretary to the Navy and was to play a leading part in its reform, wrote in his diary for 7 October 1665:

> Did business, though not much, at the office, because of the horrible crowd and lamentable moan of the poor seamen, that lie starving in the streets through lack of money, which do trouble and perplex me to the heart; and more at noon, when we were to go through them, for then above a whole hundred of them followed us; some cursing, some swearing, and some praying to us.

A few lines later, there is a grim reminder of the dangers of life ashore. 'Talking with him in the highway, come close by the bearers with a dead corpse of the plague; but Lord! to see what custom is, that I am come almost to think nothing of it'.

The ticket system was naturally a great cause of discontent, and the authorities made a curious attempt to improve morale in the fleet. This was to allow seamen to bring their wives to live aboard with them. Although this was naturally a popular move, it was often abused, many of the 'wives' being dockside prostitutes, and the inevitable result was a rapid increase in venereal disease.

Pepys' great contribution to the development of the Navy was his introduction of efficient and business-like methods. Although he industriously overhauled every aspect of the administration, the victualling or supplying of food and drink to the fleet still gave such opportunities for corruption that it was very difficult to reform. Even Pepys himself was far from guiltless in this respect. Dennis Gauden (afterwards knighted, but eventually ruined) was the Victualler to the Navy, and on Christmas Eve 1662, Pepys wrote: 'This evening Mr Gauden sent me, against Christmas, a great chine of beef and three dozen of tongues'. He also received much larger gifts from the same source, including two sums of over £500 each.

Renewal of the Dutch Wars

Trade rivalry again led to war with the Dutch and the fleet had to be prepared very quickly. Idle ships were hastily recommissioned, and the press-gang set to work in the seaports to collect as many men as they could lay their hands on. The first battle was fought off Lowestoft in 1665, and although it was not a defeat, the Duke of York lost his command and was replaced by George Monk, now Duke of Albemarle, and Prince Rupert. The following year came the Four Days' Battle, with considerable English losses, including 2,000 men taken prisoner. Pepys described how the prisoners' wives besieged the Navy Office: '... the yard being very full of women, I believe about three hundred, coming to get money for their husbands and friends; and they lay clamouring, and swearing, and cursing us ...'

Some of the prisoners agreed to serve in the Dutch fleet and were well and promptly paid. The news soon reached England, where the morale of the seamen was so low that many deserted to the Dutch, after crossing the North Sea in fishing boats and merchant ships.

What followed was the worst humiliation ever suffered by the English Navy. In June 1667, the Dutch fleet under Admiral de Ruyter appeared in the mouth of the Thames and moved up the river. The Duke of Albemarle was put in charge of the defences, and though an old man, acted very quickly. In a few days he had gun batteries and guardships in place, but the Dutch broke through, captured one of our finest ships, the *Royal Charles*, and burnt six more. Pepys reported a conversation on 14 June: 'But that, that he tells me of worse consequence is that he himself, I think he said, did hear many Englishmen aboard the Dutch ships speaking to one another in English; and that they did cry and say, "We did heretofore fight for tickets; now we fight for dollars!"'

Albemarle's guns and forts eventually forced the Dutch to retreat, but it had been a very close thing. The disgrace had, at any rate, the result of publicising the plight of the sailors, and the interval of peace which followed gave an opportunity for things to be put right.

13 The Dutch attacking Chatham, 1667

Pepys' reforms

Pepys deserves great credit for the reforms which were now put into effect, although there was one much needed change he failed to bring about. It was still easy for a nobleman or Court dandy to get a command in the Navy, and with no experience at sea, such officers were often hopelessly incompetent. Seamen have always been quick to spot an officer who does not know his job, and the appointment of these amateurs caused great resentment.

Fortunately, there were professional captains as well, who had been promoted as a result of service at sea, and who were liked and respected by their men. On a visit to a squadron at Tangier, Pepys wrote that he was horrified by the behaviour of the officers, hearing 'every day fresh instances of their debauchery'. He did his best to prevent unsuitable appointments and the number of unqualified captains was reduced. When he found such a person in command, he would write him frequent letters pointing out the regulations, asking for official reports as to why they were not obeyed, and generally harrying him until he realised that commanding a warship was not the easy berth he had imagined.

This insistence on professional standards extended to junior officers as well, and the system of putting them on half-pay when not employed was started. Not only did this system keep some inefficient officers ashore, but it gave the country a trained reserve to call upon in case of war. It was also the beginning of the opportunity to make a full career in the Navy.

For the men there was not yet the same chance, as they were taken on as volunteers or 'pressed men', for a ship's commission, which would usually last between two and five years. After that, they could volunteer for a further commission, and men would often follow a popular captain to another ship.

The reforms carried out by Pepys very greatly improved the life of the seaman. Not only was he usually better led, but he received his pay regularly, as well as a fair share of any prize money to which he was entitled. Even the victualling improved, as more care was taken to see that contracts were honestly carried out. No doubt there were still dishonest pursers aboard ship but their pay was increased so as to make it unnecessary to cheat the men in order to make a living. Pensions for disabled men and for widows, a tolerable hospital service ashore and more surgeons aboard—all these improvements made the service a more acceptable alternative to life in a squalid, unhealthy town.

Although ships were terribly overcrowded, the men now slept in hammocks and ate at tables with benches. They were divided into messes, each with its share of the deck-space between the guns. There were, of course, still difficulties about preserving food at sea. Meat was always pickled in brine, but water and biscuits soon deteriorated and cheese became stale and hard. Even so, the diet on board was better than that of the poor townspeople at the time.

Medical care aboard was rough and ready in the extreme. To become a ship's surgeon one only had to pass an oral examination by an interviewing board at the Guild of Barber-Surgeons in London. The surgeon and his assistants, known as surgeon's mates, practised in the ship's cockpit, a small compartment lit only by candles. Here they looked after the sick, with, at best, a very limited knowledge of diseases and their treatment. Operations, including the amputation of limbs, were carried out with few instruments and no regard for hygiene, and chances of survival were small indeed.

Punishment on board was still severe, though as always it depended on the humanity or otherwise of the captain. Flogging was now becoming commoner, ducking and keel-hauling (dragging a man under the ship's keel on a rope) were still carried on. The diary of a Warwickshire parson, the Rev Henry Teonge, who became a naval chaplain in 1675 to escape his creditors, contains many references to punishments, such as:

August 16, 1678. A seaman received 29 lashes with a cat of nine tails, and was then washed with salt water, for stealing our carpenter's mate's wife's ring.

He was conscientious in performing burial services, and in 1679, aboard the *Royal Oak*, he was kept constantly busy:

February 7. This day I buried out of our ship: John Parr and John Woolger. I think they were little better than starved to death with the cold weather.

February 9. I buried our captain's cabin boy, Imanuell Dearam.
February 11. I buried Samuell Ward, who had lain sick a long time.

During the voyage home from Minorca to England, the *Royal Oak* lost her captain and over 60 of her crew.

However, the sailor's life was not entirely dismal—it had its lighter side. Most ships had a band of some kind, or at least some member of the crew who could play the fiddle or some other musical instrument. There was 'dancing and skylarking' on the upper deck whenever possible, for we were still a musical nation. A singsong on the messdeck has always been popular, and there were plenty of naval ballads to choose from. 'The Sea-Martyrs; or the Seamen's Sad Lamentation for their Faithful Service, Bad Pay, and Cruel Usage' dates from about 1691:

> *Good people, do but lend an ear,*
> *And a sad story you shall hear.*
> *A sadder you never heard—*
> *Of due desert and base reward,*
> *Which will our English subjects fright*
> *For our new Government to fight.*
>
> *Our seamen are the only men,*
> *That o'er the French did vict'ry gain;*
> *They kept the foe from landing here,*
> *Which would have cost the Court full dear;*
> *And when they for their pay did hope*
> *They were rewarded with a rope.*

It continues, in many verses, to describe the plight of the unpaid sailors and their families, and tells how some of those who were bold enough to demand their pay were put to death. The ballad ends on a bitter note:

> *Where is the subject's liberty?*
> *And eke where is their property?*
> *We're forc'd to fight for naught, like slaves,*
> *And though we do, we're hang'd like knaves.*
> *This is not like Old England's ways:*
> *'New lords, new laws', the proverb says.*

This particular ballad reflects the discontent which again pervaded the service after the accession of William III, the Dutchman who succeeded James II. James had fled to France, and that country was at war with England and her new ally,

Holland. During the War of the English Succession, as it is called, the naval debt, which had been greatly reduced, mounted again, and thus the sailors' pay fell into arrears once more.

The ballads are a rough guide to the state of the Navy at the time; this cheerful and patriotic one, sung to the tune of 'A Fig for France and Holland too', dates from the Dutch Wars:

> *Ring bells for joy, let none be sad,*
> *For now we have news will make you glad,*
> *Will make you blithe and merry too,*
> *To see how the Dutch are forc'd to bow:*
> *Their brags and boasts will not prevail,*
> *We'll teach them for to lowre their sail . . .*
>   (Chorus)
> *Then Hogans Mogans*, b'ware your pates,*
> *For now we shall make you distressed states.*

This ballad shows something of the spirit which the Navy had recovered as a result of the eventual victories over the Dutch and the increased efficiency which it owed above all to Samuel Pepys. Although Pepys fell from power soon after William III became King, and the Navy went through another bad patch during the war against the French, the foundations of the modern service had been well and truly laid.

* a nickname for the Dutch.

3 War and Peace in the Eighteenth Century

Although some of the many accounts of increased corruption after Samuel Pepys' loss of office were exaggerated, there was a great increase in the number of complaints against naval captains. These complaints were usually to do with prize money or with victualling.

Prize money
Investigations over prize money were made by Commissioners and they were kept busy with these complicated affairs. Anything above the main deck of a ship, except her fittings, was 'plunder' and as such did not have to be accounted for. What was not plunder was prize, and the advantages of ignoring the distinction were obvious, so looting of cargo took place before a prize crew could be sent on board to guard it. Some captains were not above keeping for themselves 'deck plunder' (goods taken from the deck) which should have been divided among the crew. Cabin plunder, on the other hand, belonged by right to the captain and his officers.

A typical complaint concerned HMS *Falkland*, commanded by a Captain Underdown. While on convoy duty in the West Indies, she captured two French merchant ships and a frigate. On her return to England, the Prize Commissioners received a letter signed only *Falkland*. It states that

> On the 13 April 1704, we met with three French ships, of which two were taken by us, both laden with sugar, indigo and cotton, but now are very light, our Captain having taken out all he can, both between decks and hold.... We would say more, but being very severely used by our Captain and Lieutenants, we are forced to keep ourselves and not sign.... And on the 15 July 1704 took another large ship bound for Canada supposed to be worth near £100,000, we doubt not that our Captain hath £10,000 worth of goods already....'

Although Captain Underdown won his case, it was commonly believed by seamen that their officers were taking more than their share from captured ships. The men themselves, whose individual share of a prize was very small, never hesitated to seize whatever they could whenever the opportunity occurred.

Cause for complaint
As for complaints about victualling, they were still difficult to prove. One such

14 An eighteenth-century officer taking his ease: *Captain Lord George Graham in his Cabin*, by William Hogarth

was made in 1704 by Charles Hore, of 'considerable frauds and mismanagements in the victualling of Her Majesty's Navy, by which the health and lives of the seamen are in danger. An enquiry was ordered, but the surveyors appointed were unable to start their job for four months, after which delay all was found to be in 'the greatest order imaginable'. Mr Hore had better luck when he complained about the beer supplied to the fleet. His petition to the House of Commons led to an investigation in which fraud on a large scale was proved.

Another cause for complaint came in the early eighteenth century. Men were transferred from one ship to another, although they had enlisted to serve in a particular vessel. The custom was to pay a ship once a year in alphabetical order. Thus a man who was transferred just before his ship's pay day would have to wait until his new ship's day came up. He would be given a ticket showing the amount of his back pay, but it was quite common for a man to receive nothing for several years. If he pledged his ticket with a money-lender, he would get much less than its face value. Seamen's wives and children often had to exist on charity or on payments from the poor rate.

Not surprisingly, many men deserted, although they could be punished by death if caught. Desertion became such a problem that seamen were offered their back pay if they returned. For example, in 1704, it was announced in the *London Gazette*: 'Her Majesty's Ships the *Revenge, Hampton Court, Expedition* and *Warspight*, being assigned on immediate service to Portugal, and many of their men being said to be absent; These are to give notice, that it is intended to pay the ship's companies a year's wages at Spithead before they sail from thence. . . .'

During the later years of Queen Anne's reign, better times returned for the Navy. The Court fops whom Pepys had tried so hard to supersede, no longer had command of ships; the new type of professional officer was taking over. As many of them had no private means, they were dependent on their pay and prize money. Thus a great deal of time was spent at sea, cruising in search of prizes, and tedious work it was.

Naval battles in the eighteenth century

The eighteenth century was for the British Navy a succession of wars, broken by intervals of peace. In 1713 the War of the Spanish Succession ended and Britain was at peace for over 25 years. Then came the War of the Austrian Succession (1739–1748), a short spell of peace, the Seven Years' War (1756–1763), another short peace, the War of American Independence (1775–1783), and then wars against the French and Spaniards once again.

The professional officers thus had plenty of opportunity to distinguish themselves in battle. Sir George Rooke destroyed an entire enemy fleet inside the fortified harbour of La Hogue in 1702 and captured Gibraltar two years later.

15 *After the Battle of Quiberon Bay,* 1759. This painting gives a good idea of the dangerous rocks and shoals

16 Admiral Lord Hood

Admiral Vernon made a successful cruise to the West Indies in 1739 and seized the Spanish stronghold of Porto Bello. Admiral George Anson sailed round the world and returned in 1744 with a captured Spanish treasure galleon and other booty valued at about £750,000. Rich prizes again resulted from his victory over the French fleet off Finisterre in 1747, for which he was raised to the peerage. During the Seven Years' War, Boscawen and Rodney destroyed a French squadron and a fleet of flat-bottomed invasion boats, while Hawke kept the French fleet bottled up by blockading their harbour of Brest. Between them they freed England from the first serious invasion threat since the Armada, and when the Brest fleet eventually put to sea, Hawke attacked. Two French ships were sunk, two more surrendered, and most of the rest were driven on to the rocks by the November gale, while Hawke's ships rode safely at anchor. This battle of Quiberon Bay was shortly followed by another off the Portuguese coast, the battle of Lagos. Here Admiral Edward Boscawen, in command of the Mediterranean fleet, chased the French, who lost five ships in the action, and prevented them from reaching Brest.

The most decisive victory of all was the battle of the Saints in 1782. The French had come in on the side of the American colonies, and they had a powerful fleet under Admiral de Grasse in the West Indies. De Grasse put to sea in an attempt to invade the British colony of Jamaica and was met by an equal force under Admiral Rodney. In the battle which followed, Rodney broke through the French line in two places and captured five ships, including de Grasse's flagship. His second-in-command, Admiral Hood, took two more, but to Hood's disgust, Rodney broke off the action and failed to take the chance of completely destroying the French fleet. Hood felt so strongly about this that he wrote in a letter to a

17 A ship on the stocks in a naval dockyard

friend at the Admiralty: 'Had I, my dear friend, had the honour of commanding his Majesty's noble fleet on the 12th, I may, without the imputation of much vanity, say the Flag of England should now have graced the stern of *upwards* of twenty sail of the enemy's ships of the line'.

The officers

There were more peaceful achievements too. Captain James Cook, who rose from the lower deck by sheer ability, made two important voyages of discovery to Australia, New Zealand and the Pacific islands.

The victorious admirals of the eighteenth century became national figures, and like their Elizabethan predecessors, found no lack of men ready to follow them. Vernon's expedition to the West Indies came at the end of a long period of peace, when, as usual, the Navy had been allowed to run down. His squadron therefore contained an unusually high proportion of victims of the press-gang. It says much for Vernon that these men fought as bravely as any volunteer could have done. A letter written by one of them to his wife (one of the earliest known

18 A purser in the eighteenth-century Navy

letters from a seaman) tells how 'we have taken Porto Belo with such coridge and bravery that i never saw before'. He often refers to Admiral Vernon as 'our dear Admiral' and recounts that 'he ordered every man some Spanish Dollers to be immediately given which is like a Man of Honour'. Soon afterwards, when Chagres, another Spanish stronghold, was taken, Vernon once more ordered an immediate distribution of prize money, although it was completely against the regulations.

As their reputation grew, these officers did not need the press-gang to make up their crews. When Boscawen paid off his ship, the *Namur*, in 1758, he was able to inform the Admiralty that almost all the ship's company had volunteered to serve with him for another commission. An incident during the next year gives a clue to one reason why seamen were so keen to serve under his command. In an action against the French, Boscawen's flagship was disabled and unable to keep up the pursuit of the enemy. He ordered his barge to be launched so that he could transfer to another ship, the *Newark*. On the way his barge was holed by an enemy shot, so Boscawen snatched off his wig, plugged the hole and reached the *Newark* amid the cheers of her crew.

19 A seaman in the eighteenth-century Navy

Unhealthy conditions

Although the Navy was at war for a substantial part of the eighteenth century, it is certain that more men were killed by disease than by enemy action. The reasons were the same as before—crowded conditions, lack of knowledge, or neglect, of hygiene, and lack of fresh provisions. Disease was particularly rife in the fleet at this time, as for the first time, many ships were serving on tropical stations for long spells.

A particularly disastrous example of the effects of tropical service was the expedition to the West Indies under Admiral Francis Hosier in 1726. Although Hosier was a humane officer, his ships were allowed to become so foul and insanitary that the crews died like flies. The admiral himself and his two successors succumbed, and altogether of his force of 4,600, less than 600 survived. Hosier's body was buried in the ballast of his flagship, spreading the disease still further, until months later it was sent to England in a homeward bound vessel.

For a horrifying account of the unhealthy conditions on the West Indies station there is the evidence of the Letters of Captain Edward Thompson, describing conditions at Antigua in 1756:

> I officiate as chaplain, and bury 8 men in a morning. Fluxes [dysentery] and fevers are the reigning distemper, and both I attribute to the water drunk by the seamen, which is taken out of tanks or cisterns, built by Admiral Knowles. It is all rain water, and covered close up, which, for want of air, breeds poisonous animalculae, and becomes foul and putrid. The melancholy effect it produces might be in a great manner prevented by boiling the water before it is issued, or ordering the people to do it. This would destroy the vermin and correct the putrefaction. I am convinced from long observation that most of the distempers in southern climates arise from the water drunk, as ship sicknesses do from the bilge waters, which is evidently proved in leaky ships being always healthful. I therefore recommend all officers, naval and mercantile, to let in salt water every day, and boil their water fresh, for the good of themselves and cargoes.

20 A captain in the eighteenth-century Navy

Scurvy

This indicates that neglect rather than ignorance was the main cause of much disease at sea. On long voyages, however, the great scourge was still scurvy, and for a long time it was believed that there was no cure for this disease. The idea that salt meat was the cause was disproved during Anson's voyage round the world. When his ship the *Centurion* crossed the Pacific, the crew lived on fresh fish and livestock and drank fresh water, yet the average death rate from scurvy was twelve men a day.

On the other hand, during Captain Cook's voyages, the disease was almost unknown. This was due to Cook's great care over the quality and storage of food, for he was passionately concerned for the health of his men. He particularly believed in the value of pickled cabbage (sauerkraut), and regularly ate it as an example to his crew. He was also ahead of his time in his insistence on cleanliness, fumigation and ventilation between decks and the airing of bedding.

Even in Elizabethan days, scurvy had been prevented by Captain James Lancaster on a voyage to Sumatra in 1601, when he gave his crew a daily dose of lemon juice. They survived while men in other ships sickened and died. In 1616 on a voyage to find the North West Passage, lime juice was carried in the ships. Later on, in the eighteenth century, the East India Company's ships always carried a large stock of lemons, and scurvy was uncommon compared with its incidence in the Navy.

In 1754 a naval surgeon called James Lind published a *Treatise on Scurvy*, in which he gave the cure, but even then the Admiralty took no effective action. Some captains certainly acted on his advice, but many thousands of seamen died before scurvy was finally conquered in the Navy.

During the eighteenth century, the Navy's numbers oscillated rapidly. In times of peace they were down to 12,000 or 13,000; in the first year of the Seven Years' War, they rose to 60,000 and by the end there were 116,000 men serving. Numbers could only be raised at this rate by the press-gang. Recruiting posters, in spite of their tempting promises of prize money and 'a bountiful supply of clothing, beef, grog, flip, and strong beer', could never bring in enough men to man the wartime fleet.

Newly-pressed men were first sent to a seaport, where they were hustled aboard a tender and kept under guard with hatches battened down, until transferred to a receiving ship for drafting to the fleet. In both the tenders and the receiving ships, conditions were appallingly insanitary. Overcrowding was much worse than in normal ships, and as many of the pressed men were diseased or verminous, preservation of health was practically impossible.

The surgeons who examined the men in the receiving ships often reported to the Admiralty on the necessity for washing them on arrival and issuing them with new uniforms. Nothing effective was done and many of the sudden outbreaks of typhus which spread rapidly through the fleet in the eighteenth century were caused by neglect of the surgeons' recommendations.

21 The Moonlight Battle, 1780, in which Admiral Rodney's fleet captured six Spanish ships

The man most responsible for improving the health of seamen was Sir Gilbert Blane, who went to the West Indies in 1779 as personal physician to Admiral Rodney. He was more fortunate than Lind, as owing to Rodney's influence, he was made Physician to the Fleet, and when in 1781 he presented his *Memorial* to the Admiralty, their Lordships took notice. There was nothing particularly new new in Blane's ideas, and much of what he wrote had already been noted by the neglected Lind. Blane's first point was insistence on the importance of keeping ships clean, dry and well ventilated and the men clean, dry and properly clothed. Fresh drinking water, oranges, lemons, limes and fresh vegetables were specifically mentioned as the means for preventing and curing scurvy. 'Every fifty oranges or lemons might be considered as a hand to the fleet, inasmuch as the health, and perhaps the life, of a man would thereby be saved'.

Those officers who cared for the welfare of their men were amply repaid by loyalty and devotion. Boscawen was a notable example and we have already seen how nearly all his ship's company volunteered for a new commission with him.

Hawke's victory at Quiberon Bay was due, not only to superb seamanship, but also to his meticulous care for the health and welfare of his crews. During the arduous blockade of Brest which preceded the battle, Hawke was writing constantly to the Admiralty for fresh victuals. He succeeded in goading their Lordships to action, and four special transport ships were fitted out and sent to Plymouth. They went to and fro, supplying the fleet with live cattle and sheep for slaughtering as well as 'cabbages, turnips, carrots, potatoes and onions', not forgetting a regular supply of beer. The result was that when the French fleet came out, Hawke's crews cheered as they manned their guns in the November gale, among the dangerous shoals and rocks of Quiberon Bay.

During the next year, 1760, Boscawen relieved Hawke off Brest, and the good health of the crews was maintained. Boscawen occupied an island off the French coast and sent men ashore as gardeners to grow a supply of fresh vegetables from seed he himself paid for.

Naval victories like Quiberon Bay can only be won by disciplined and welltrained men, skilfully led. The standard of gunnery in the British fleet was very high; on the average, the French fired three times as many broadsides, with much less effect. British gunners were trained to hold their fire until they were well within range, irrespective of what the enemy was doing, and to aim at his hull rather than at his rigging, as the French did. Seamanship training was equally important in those days of sailing ships—not only the handling of sails but speedy repair of rigging damaged during an action.

Discipline
As for discipline, it was always strict and often harsh. Boscawen himself punished with severity any man who committed the slightest offence. The eighteenth century was a brutal age, and the use of the horrible whip called the cat of nine tails had become general in the Navy. The captain of a ship was not allowed by regulation to order more than twelve lashes, but Boscawen often broke this rule, as did most captains; when he became an admiral and presided at courtsmartial, Boscawen was even more severe, and would order as many as 500 lashes. In 1747, for example, there was a mutiny aboard his former command, the *Namur* and 57 men were charged. Boscawen condemned 3 to be hanged and 12 to receive from 100 to 500 lashes.

American War of Independence
So far we have seen the eighteenth century as mainly a period of success in naval warfare and some improvement in conditions afloat. Unfortunately, after the end of the Seven Years' War, a general deterioration set in, with men paid off and ships badly maintained. The interval before the War of American Independence was only twelve years, but much harm had been done. The Navy once again was

22 The press-gang in action, 1779

unprepared, and this time it was called upon to fight an unpopular war. There was a great deal of sympathy among British seamen for the Americans in their fight for independence, as well as a natural reluctance to go to war with those whom they regarded as their fellow countrymen.

There was also a great deterioration in the quality of the officers. The generation which produced Hawke and Boscawen was no longer active, and the next generation of outstanding leaders had not yet arrived on the scene. Lack of success in the early stages of the war, and the consequent lack of prize money, led to even lower morale in the fleet. Official statistics of the years 1774 to 1780 showed that during that period 175,900 men had been enlisted in the Navy. Of these only 1,243 were killed in action, while 18,541 died of sickness or disease. The number of deserters reached the staggering total of 42,069—a comment on the unpopularity of the service to which nothing need be added.

It is true that when the French and Spaniards, our traditional enemies, joined the war on the American side in 1778, something of the old fighting spirit returned, especially towards the end, with Rodney's victory over the French in the Battle of the Saints. In this engagement, when Rodney's flagship, the *Formidable*, broke the enemy's line, his gunners held their fire as usual until the precise moment when it would be most effective. The cheers of the British crews as they went into action were said to have almost drowned the sound of gunfire. Rodney's flag captain, Sir Charles Douglas, noted the contrast in discipline between British and French crews after the French flagship struck her colours in token of surrender: 'The moment the *Ville de Paris* struck, her worthless and disorderly crew broke open the chests and trunks of all their officers, and with lighted candles in their hands stave in the doors of the store rooms in quest of wine and other strong liquors .. notwithstanding some thousands of land forces having been on board the French fleet, only one single musket, to the best of my recollection, was fired at the *Formidable*'.

However, in those days the fleet was operating mainly in the West Indies which, until Sir Gilbert Blane's recommendations were acted upon, was a notoriously unhealthy station. Blane's book, *Observations on the Diseases of Seamen*, gives the figures of deaths and sickness for the month of March 1782. Twenty-seven men died, only one of wounds, the rest from disease, 1,884 men reported sick, 804 with fever and 463 with flux (dysentery).

Once again, however, better days were not far ahead. Towards the end of the century, many of the officers who were soon to win lasting fame were already beginning to make their mark. Nelson himself, the greatest of them all, was promoted captain in 1778, at the age of twenty.

4 The Napoleonic Wars

In 1793, ten years after the American War, the British Navy once again found itself fighting the French. The French King and Queen had been imprisoned and later executed and a revolutionary Government set up; in 1792 France attacked Holland, and early in the following year declared war on Britain.

Our Navy had, as usual, been allowed to run down, but the results were less serious than on previous occasions. The principal reason was that for half the spell of peace the First Lord of the Admiralty was a sea-going officer, Admiral Lord Howe. He managed, in his five years of office before the outbreak of war, to get an average budget of £1,300,000—nearly twice the sum allowed in the last period of peace.

Manning the ships

Thus in 1793 we were better prepared than usual, although men were needed—and quickly. Volunteers were better than pressed men, and great efforts were made to induce them to join. The royal bounty of 30 shillings (£1.50) was given in addition to pay when signing on, and further bounties were offered by seaports and cities. In 1793, the City of London gave 40 shillings (£2) to an able seaman and 20 shillings (£1) to an ordinary seaman who enlisted voluntarily. Later this was increased to 10 guineas (£10.50) for an ordinary seaman, and some seaports offered as much as £30 to an able seaman. The snag about this system was that a man could take the bounty in one town, desert as soon as possible, and then enlist elsewhere under another name to claim a second bounty. Also, the large sums offered were a temptation to men who might soon prove to be unsuited to the hard life aboard a naval ship.

A useful source of recruits was the Marine Society, which had been founded in 1756. Its original purpose was to take poor boys from the town streets, fit them out with clothing and enlist them in the Navy. It now concerned itself also with men, who were enrolled as landsmen (at 16 shillings [80p] a month) until they were sufficiently skilled to become ordinary seamen. During the period of these wars against France, the Marine Society supplied over 20,000 men to the Navy.

In spite of the bounty system and the press-gang (which was always active), the demand for men exceeded the supply, and other methods had to be tried. In 1795, the Quota Act was passed by Parliament; it made each county in England and Wales responsible for providing a certain number of men for the Navy, in proportion to its population. The Act was soon extended to the seaports, and this

23 A recruiting poster from the Napoleonic Wars. The scale of bounties shows how badly men were needed

VOLUNTEERS.

G.   R. III.

God Save the King.

LET us, who are Englishmen, protect and defend our good KING and COUNTRY against the Attempts of all *Republicans* and *Levellers*, and against the Designs of our NATURAL ENEMIES, who intend in this Year to invade OLD ENGLAND, *our happy Country*, to murder our gracious KING as they have done *their own*; to make WHORES of our *Wives* and *Daughters*; to rob us of our Property, and teach us nothing but the *damn'd Art of murdering one another.*

ROYAL TARS Of OLD ENGLAND,

If you love your COUNTRY, and your LIBERTY, now is the Time to shew your Love.

REPAIR,

All who have good Hearts, who love their KING, their COUNTRY, and RELIGION, who hate the FRENCH, and damn the POPE,

TO

Lieut. W. J. Stephens,

At his Rendezvous, SHOREHAM,

Where they will be allowed to Enter for any SHIP of WAR,

AND THE FOLLOWING

BOUNTIES will be given by his MAJESTY, in Addition to Two Months Advance.

To Able Seamen,	*Five Pounds.*
To Ordinary Seamen,	*Two Pounds Ten Shillings.*
To Landmen,	*Thirty Shillings.*

Conduct-Money paid to go by Land, and their Chests and Bedding sent Carriage free.
Those Men who have served as PETTY-OFFICERS, and those who are otherwise qualified, will be recommended accordingly.

LEWES: PRINTED BY W. AND A. LEE.

meant that larger numbers were brought in. They were known as Lord Mayors' men, because many of them had been sent for trial for one offence or another, and given the choice of joining the Navy or going to prison. This system was widely used by local authorities as a means of making up their quota. Naturally, Lord Mayors' men were unpopular aboard, being regarded as riff-raff who had only joined to escape gaol. Many of them were filthy and covered in lice, and often they had a larger bounty than genuine volunteers.

It has been estimated that the average ship's company of the time was made up of nearly one-half pressed men and nearly one-third volunteers. The rest were Lord Mayors' men and foreigners of various nationalities, in roughly equal numbers. It is surprising to find such a large number of foreigners serving in British warships; the *Victory* at the battle of Trafalgar carried 71 (including Frenchmen!) and many ships had even larger numbers. Most of them would have been picked up by the press-gang in seaports, where they were conspicuous and an easy prey.

This motley collection of men was responsible for some of the greatest victories at sea in all British history. The main reason was that, generally speaking, they were exceptionally well led by officers genuinely concerned for their welfare. The greatest of these was Nelson, but there were among his captains, his 'band of brothers', as he called them, many who were outstandingly able and humane. Most of them came from good, but not aristocratic, country families; Nelson himself was the son of a country parson in Norfolk.

Nelson's early career
Nelson had an extraordinary capacity for inspiring affection, and was equally loved by officers and men. When he rejoined the fleet before the battle of Trafalgar, an officer wrote: 'Lord Nelson is arrived, and a sort of general joy has been the consequence'. When the crew of Nelson's barge (an Admiral's personal boat) heard that he was to leave his flagship, the *Foudroyant*, they wrote him this most moving letter:

My Lord, It is with extreme grief that we find you are about to leave us. We have been along with you (although not in the same ship) in every Engagement your Lordship has been in, both by Sea and Land; and most humbly beg of Your Lordship to permit us to go to England, as your Boat's crew, in any Ship or Vessel, or in any way that may seem most pleasing to Your Lordship. My Lord, pardon the rude style of Seamen, who are but little acquainted with writing, and believe us to be, my Lord, your ever humble and obedient servants.

The first victories against the French were won under the command of the older generation of admirals. In 1794 Richard Howe followed the enemy fleet

24 The Battle of the Glorious First of June, 1794: Lord Howe (Black Dick) on the quarterdeck of the *Queen Chnrlotte*

into the Atlantic, broke through it, captured six ships and sank one. The French were commanded by Admiral Villaret-Joyeuse, who had been a junior officer until the Revolution and one of the few officers who survived it. He proved himself worthy of his rapid promotion as a very able commander. Howe, on the other hand, had been in the Navy for over 50 years and had already served in four wars. The Glorious First of June, as it is always called, was a great victory, though if Howe had been younger and more vigorous, it could have been an even more crushing defeat for the French. As it was, they lost seven ships, but Howe was unable to prevent their supplies of corn from America from getting through.

The next notable victory was three years later and at a time when it was very much needed. We were by now fighting the Spaniards and Dutch as well as the French, and our Mediterranean fleet, under Sir John Jervis, had been driven out into the Atlantic.

Jervis sighted the Spanish fleet off Cape St Vincent one day in February 1797. He had only 15 ships against the enemy's 27, but he knew they were on their way to meet the French fleet at Brest—and he knew he had to stop them. What he did was to cut the Spanish fleet into two parts and then prevent them from joining up again. This bold plan would have failed if Nelson had not taken his ship, the *Captain*, off without orders to hold the gap open (by engaging 17 enemy ships at once) until the rest of the British fleet came up. After the battle, Commodore Nelson went aboard the flagship, not certain what reception he would get. He need not have worried, for the usually stern Jervis embraced him and thanked him for his part in the victory.

It was a decisive part, as Nelson had again distinguished himself by first attacking the *Santissima Trinidad*, said to be the largest ship in the world, and then leading boarding parties to capture two enemy vessels. Nelson's friend Collingwood did well too, as he captured two ships with the *Excellent*. There was great rejoicing at home, Jervis was made Earl St Vincent and Nelson promoted Rear-Admiral.

Mutinies

Before the next important victory, Camperdown, in 1797, a most extraordinary thing had happened. The fleet at Spithead mutinied, followed by the ships at the Nore. The war was by now going badly; the French had tried to invade Ireland, and had been prevented, not by the British Navy, but by bad weather. Napoleon was steadily overrunning Europe, and there were fears that he would invade Britain.

25 Richard Parker, President of the Committee of Delegates, tendering the List of Grievances to Vice Admiral Buckner on Board the *Sandwich* at the Nore

Thus the mutinies could not have come at a worse time for the country's morale. They were caused by widespread discontent throughout the service, shown by a number of petitions from the lower deck to the Admiralty in the early stages of the war. These were often complaints of brutal treatment; the crew of the *Nassau*, for example, wrote in 1795: 'It is almost impossible for us to put it down in paper as cruel as it really is with flogging and abusing'.

It was pay, however, which was the main grievance leading to mutinies. Rates of pay had, incredibly enough, not been increased since Cromwell's time, 150 years before. It was still subject to deductions such as the contribution to the Chatham Chest and there were often delays of as much as two years in paying a ship's crew.

Petitions on this subject, in reasonable and indeed respectful language, were sent from each ship at Spithead to the Admiralty but were completely ignored. Fresh petitions were addressed to Lord Howe, who was at Bath, recovering from an attack of gout. Howe, over 70 and practically retired, handed them over to the Admiralty; althouth their Lordships discussed the matter, they did nothing.

26 Admiral Lord Duncan

27 The Battle of the Nile, 1798. The French fleet at anchor in Aboukir Bay is approached by Nelson's force

Naturally, the men were embittered by official indifference to their reasonable requests. Their next move was to send further petitions to the Admiralty, and this time, copies to Charles James Fox, Leader of the Opposition in Parliament. At last Lord Bridport, who had taken over command of the Channel Fleet from Howe, got to know what was going on, and at once realised it was very serious. By now it was too late, as the mutiny had already been planned.

The Admiralty, even now showing a complete lack of understanding of the situation, ordered the fleet to sea, but the crews refused to obey their officers. A committee (two delegates from each ship) was elected to draw up rules for running the fleet. Some officers were allowed to remain on board, while other (usually the unpopular ones) were sent ashore. Officers were treated with respect and their orders obeyed, watches were kept as usual, and there were several penalties for drunkenness.

Lieutenant Beaver of the *Monarch* wrote: 'The seamen still continue to conduct themselves incredibly well, performing their usual duties with alacrity, and behaving towards their officers with the greatest respect. I had always great respect for an English seaman; I like the character now better than ever'.

Even now Parliament and the Admiralty were slow and indecisive. They offered a very small increase in pay, but the sailors made it clear that they wanted better food, better pensions, fair treatment aboard, and a pardon from the King for all the fleet. Until these demands were granted, they would not go to sea.

The pardon was signed by King George III and read out by Lord Bridport in his flagship, with a promise that the other demands would be met. A fortnight later, however, the necessary Act of Parliament had not been passed, and the men were thoroughly impatient. Then the Admiralty, with incredible stupidity, sent a disciplinary order to all captains, instructing them to quell the mutiny. Although this was supposed to be read out to the lower deck, the officers sensibly kept it to themselves and did nothing. However, rumours of it got around, as rumours always do in ships, and made the situation worse. In the *London* there was a scuffle in which a number of men and two officers were killed.

At last Parliament acted; the Bill was rushed through and a messenger galloped to Portsmouth with a copy. But there was still another complication. The disciplinary order from the Admiralty had made another pardon necessary. Lord Howe was sent for once again and given a free hand. The indomitable old man went from ship to ship until he was so exhausted that he had to be lifted ashore. The most difficult question was the dismissal of brutal officers, which had been demanded by the delegates from the first. Howe dismissed 59 officers, including an admiral and four captains. The royal pardon arrived, and Black Dick was carried through Portsmouth on the shoulders of the delegates, amid cheering crowds. The Admiral invited the delegates to dinner and all was over. Both officers and men kept honourably to the terms of the agreement, and nobody was victimised or punished in any way.

28 Lord Nelson: the famous portrait by Lemuel Abbott

The second mutiny, at the Nore, which had already started, was a very different affair. It was led by a most unusual man, Richard Parker, a former midshipman who had been discharged on medical grounds. After a spell as a schoolmaster, he had rejoined the Navy as a seaman under the Lord Mayors' scheme to avoid a debtors' prison. The Nore mutiny continued after the Spithead settlement, the main demands being a fairer distribution of prize money and a revision of the Articles of War, the antiquated disciplinary rules. However, the Nore fleet was on its own, and one by one the ships dropped away until only the *Sandwich*, with Parker aboard, was left. This time the pardon did not include the leaders, and when *Sandwich* surrendered, most of them were arrested. After a court-martial, 30 of them, including Parker, were hanged. The mutineers had been more or less starved out, as troops had been stationed ashore to prevent any of them landing for stores.

Even after the Nore mutineers had been executed, there was still trouble, sometimes stirred up by Irishmen, of whom there were many in the Navy. Admiral Duncan, who was waiting for the Dutch fleet to leave harbour, found even his own flagship in a mutinous condition. The Admiral, a huge man and immensely strong, picked up the ringleader and held him over the side with one hand, saying, 'My lads, look at this fellow, he who dares to deprive me of the command of the fleet'. There was no more mutiny in Duncan's command.

During the period of the Nore mutiny, Duncan's fleet had been so reduced that he had to bluff the Dutch by appearing off their coast with his only loyal ship and making signals to the non-existent remainder. The Dutch did not know what a chance they were missing, and only put to sea after the fleet had returned to normal.

What followed was the battle of Camperdown, fiercely fought and with many killed and wounded on both sides. Duncan and the Dutch Admiral de Winter each had 16 ships, although the Dutch were smaller and less powerfully armed. Half the Dutch fleet was captured, including the flagship. The fighting was so close that de Winter, who was almost as tall as Duncan, is said to have remarked afterwards, 'It is a matter of marvel that two such gigantic objects as Admiral Duncan and myself should have escaped the general carnage of the day'. It is pleasant to know that Duncan was soon on terms of warm friendship with the captured Dutch officers.

Nelson and the Theseus
We last heard of Nelson when he was promoted Rear-Admiral at the age of 39 after the battle of Cape St Vincent, in this same year of the mutinies and of Camperdown. His next ship after the *Captain* was the *Theseus*; when he joined her, he found a mutinous crew and a ship with hardly any stores. At once he busied himself in arranging supplies, including fresh vegetables, for the crew. When Nelson had been aboard for less than a fortnight, a piece of paper was found on the quarterdeck, which read, 'Success attend Admiral Nelson. God

29 The gun deck of HMS *Victory* as it is today

bless Captain Miller. We thank them for the officers they have placed over us. We are happy and comfortable, and will shed every drop of blood in our veins, and the name of the *Theseus* shall be immortalised as high as the *Captain's*'. It was signed 'Ship's Company'.

The *Theseus* was soon to be tested in action, as Nelson was ordered to Tenerife to seize Spanish treasure on the island. He had an adequate force of ships, but not the soldiers he had asked for. Nevertheless, he managed to land parties of sailors and marines, who fought their way into the town of Santa Cruz. Nelson was severely wounded in the right arm and had to have it clumsily amputated by his ship's surgeon. Meanwhile the landing party had found the town heavily defended and had been allowed by the Spanish Governor to withdraw under a flag of truce.

Nelson and the Vanguard
Nelson was in great pain from his wound and unusually depressed at the failure of the expedition, though Jervis met him with encouraging words and sent him to England on sick leave. By the following spring he was back, this time in the *Vanguard*, looking for the French fleet in the Mediterranean. After narrowly missing them several times, he found them anchored in Aboukir Bay, near the mouth of the Nile. At dusk he attacked, and within a few hours had destroyed or captured 13 of the enemy's force. It was a tremendous victory, as Nelson himself said, 'a conquest', and hailed as such by the British people. Nelson, who had been wounded in the head during the battle, was made a baron, Lord Nelson of the Nile, and medals and promotions were liberally handed out. Nelson was also given the title of Duke of Bronte by the King of Sicily, and when he returned to London, his carriage was pulled through the City by cheering people while thousands more waved from the pavements.

Nelson's next great victory was the battle of Copenhagen in 1801, when he was second-in-command to Sir Hyde Parker. The fleet was sent to attack the Danes, who with the Swedes and Russians, had been resisting the British claim to search their ships for French goods. After an attempt at peaceful settlement had failed, Nelson led the attack. Like the Nile battle, this was a very bloody affair; indeed Nelson wrote of it, 'I have been in 105 engagements, and today is the most terrible of them all'. It was during this battle that Admiral Parker gave the signal to break off the action and Nelson put his telescope to his blind eye. As a result of his disobedience, most of the Danish fleet was destroyed. Very soon afterwards the Mediterranean fleet under Admiral Sir James Saumarez fought a successful action against a combined French and Spanish fleet off Algeciras, near Gibraltar.

Naval battles against the French
In the following year, a peace treaty was signed with the French. This did not last long, as Napoleon was obviously making preparations to attack England, and in May 1803 Britain again declared war. Preparations for a French invasion were well advanced, and it was essential to keep the French Mediterranean fleet from reaching the Channel. Nelson spent the next two years almost continuously at sea watching Toulon, where the French ships under Admiral Villeneuve were waiting for an opportunity to escape. It was not until May 1805 that Nelson heard that the enemy fleet had slipped out.

Villeneuve's orders were to decoy Nelson to the West Indies, dash back to Spain (now in the war on the French side), pick up reinforcements, and guard the Channel while Napoleon's armies invaded Britain. Nelson followed the French all the way to the Caribbean and back to Gibraltar. Villeneuve, anxious to avoid

30 In this French picture of Trafalgar, the *Redoutable* is fighting Nelson's *Victory* and the *Téméraire* at the same time, at very close quarters

our Channel fleet, anchored in Vigo Bay, on the Atlantic coast of Spain. Napoleon gave up the idea of invasion and marched against Austria instead.

Nelson went home for a short leave, his first for over two years, and was cheered by large crowds wherever he went. One of his former officers met him in London and wrote: 'He was then very ill and neither in look nor dress betokened the naval hero, having on a pair of drab-green breeches, and high black gaiters, a yellow waistcoat, and a plain blue coat, with a cocked hat, quite square, a large green shade over the eye and a gold headed stick in his hand; yet the crowd ran before him and said, as he looked down, that he was then thinking of burning a fleet....'

Nelson returned to the fleet soon afterwards and called his captains aboard his flagship, the *Victory*, to tell them his plan of attack. This was to divide his force into three, two to break the enemy's line and the third to support them as necessary. He told them to act independently if the occasion called for it, as 'nothing is sure in a sea-fight'.

The combined French and Spanish fleet of 33 ships put to sea on 19 October

31 HMS *Victory* at Trafalgar: Nelson mortally wounded by a French sharpshooter

32 Aboard a British warship in 1820

1805 and Nelson went after them. He came up with them off Cape Trafalgar and gave orders for his 27 ships to form two columns, having given up his original idea of three owing to lack of numbers.

His famous signal 'England expects that every man will do his duty' was hoisted amid the cheers of the fleet. Nelson led one column and his friend Collingwood the other. The fighting was again fierce and at very close quarters. A seaman in the *Revenge* afterwards wrote his memoirs under the name of 'Jack Nastyface'. Here is part of his description of the battle:

A Spanish three-decker ran her bowsprit over our poop, with a number of her crew in it, and in her fore rigging, two or three hundred men were ready to follow; but they caught a Tartar, for their design was discovered and our marines with their small arms and carronades on the poop, loaded with canister shot, swept them off so fast, some into the water and some on the decks that they were glad to sheer off. While this was going on aft, we were engaged with a French two-deck ship on our starboard side, and on our larboard bow another, so that many of their shots must have struck their own ships, and done severe execution. After (our) being engaged about an hour, two other ships fortunately came up, received some of the fire intended for us and we were now enabled to get at some of the shot-holes between wind and water and plug them up.... We were now unable to work the ship, our yards,

33 An innocent man is about to be flogged when the real culprit confesses. This scene was depicted by George Cruickshank (famous as an illustrator of Charles Dickens's novels)

sails and masts being disabled and the braces completely shot away. In this condition we lay by the side of the enemy, firing away and now and then we received a good raking from them passing under our stern.

The battle lasted from about noon until about 5 o'clock. The French and Spaniards fought as bravely as the British, and there were many casualties. The *Royal Sovereign's* first broadside killed or wounded more than half the crew of the French *Fougeux*. The *Redoubtable*, with a ship's company of 600, had 490 killed and 81 wounded.

It was a sniper from the rigging of this last ship who gave Nelson his death wound. The dying Admiral was carried below, and survived long enough to hear that 14 of the enemy ships had surrendered. He had had a presentiment that he would not survive the battle; the previous evening he had dined with a party of midshipmen and said to them, 'Tomorrow I will do that which will give you young gentlemen something to talk and think about for the rest of your lives. But I shall not live to know about it myself'. He had also said that he would not be satisfied with less than 20 enemy ships as prizes. In fact 18 were taken during the battle; 4 more escaped only to surrender to Sir Richard Strachan a fortnight later. The rest reached Cadiz harbour and never went to sea again.

34 HMS *Warrior*, launched in 1860, was Britain's first armoured battleship. This photograph shows her at Plymouth, with the wooden two-decker *Implacable* just visible on the right

Trafalgar was the last great battle fought by sailing ships. It convinced Napoleon that it would be useless to challenge the British again at sea, and during the remaining ten years of the war, only minor actions were fought between the two Navies.

5 Trafalgar to Scapa Flow

The final defeat of Napoleon at Waterloo in 1815 began the longest period of peace in our history. It began as always with a rapid run-down of the Navy, from 140,000 men in 1813 to only 19,000 four years later. The result was not completely disastrous for the officers, who had their half-pay, but for the sailors it usually meant unemployment and poverty.

Conditions in the Navy had improved greatly during the Napoleonic wars. Pay was increased after the mutinies, food was better, with fresh meat and vegetables more often obtained at ports of call, and medical attention on board showing marked improvement. Properly ventilated sick bays on the upper deck had been introduced from 1794 onwards, though they were not universal until 1815.

In spite of these improvements, and the threat of unemployment ashore, naval service was generally unpopular. Not long after the end of the war, Lord Exmouth led an expedition against the Algerian pirates, and it was only with some difficulty that the ships were fully manned. The day of the press-gang was over in home ports (though it had not been formally abolished) and the Navy was now dependent on volunteers.

35 A *Punch* cartoon of 1912, depicting Winston Churchill talking with the ghost of Sir Richard Grenville, the Elizabethan seadog. The caption read:

A SEA-CHANGE

First Lord of the Admiralty (at Earls Court): 'Well things have changed since your time; but our lower deck's as good as ever.'
Shade of Sir Richard Grenville (of the *Revenge*): 'Yes; and I hear they're underpaid as well as ever.'

36 The stoke hole of HMS *Blenheim* in 1892. The furnaces were overhung with six vast boilers to power the engines.

Policing the sea

The Algiers expedition, which did much to stop the slave trade in that area, was typical of the Navy's new role. It had been living on the matchless reputation it won at Trafalgar, for the French fleet never put to sea again during the last ten years of the war. In 1812 Britain was briefly at war with the Americans as a result of our boarding their ships to look for deserters, press-ganging their men in foreign ports, and generally attempting to prevent them from trading with France. There were a number of single ship actions, and within a few months five British ships had surrendered to the small but highly efficient United States Navy. This disgrace was to some extent countered when the *Shannon*, after a short but bloody fight, took the surrender of the crack American frigate *Chesapeake*.

The Navy's reputation recovered further after the Algiers expedition and Admiral Codrington's part in the victory of Navarino in 1827. This time we were fighting alongside the French, and also the Russians; against us were the Turks and the Egyptians. The Turks at that time ruled Greece, and the Greeks were struggling for their independence. In an effort to enforce an armistice the combined fleets were sent to the eastern Mediterranean, and in the resulting battle, the last to be fought by sailing ships, the Turkish and Egyptian fleets were totally destroyed.

During most of the nineteenth century, the British Navy kept to its new role of policing the seas. It did valuable work in surveying uncharted waters and in stamping out the slave trade in West Africa and elsewhere. There were a great many half-pay officers, however, and not very many ships. The chance of getting to sea was slender, and opportunities for promotion smaller still. The only way of attracting an Admiral's attention was by the smart appearance of one's ship. 'Spit and polish' and severe punishment for trivial offences became the general rules. The cat o'nine tails was used freely, and as late as the 1850s a young officer in the *Albion* recorded that nearly every week a man would receive three or four dozen lashes.

Steamships

However, great changes were on the way during the long peace of the nineteenth century. The sailing ship was very gradually replaced by steam, and wooden ships by iron; gunnery, in its infancy in Nelson's day, became vastly more accurate and scientific.

The first steamship was ordered for the Royal Navy in 1822, but six years later, Lord Melville, as First Lord of the Admiralty, wrote that their Lordships considered 'that the introduction of steam is calculated to strike a fatal blow to the naval supremacy of the Empire'. One of Lord Melville's colleagues, Admiral Sir George Cockburn, could not bear to look at a steamship and remarked that since their introduction he had never seen a clean deck or a captain who did not look like a chimneysweep. Even a passion for clean decks could not stand up for ever against the advantages of steam, and by 1880 more steamships than sailing vessels were being built in British yards.

The introduction of steam made necessary a new branch of the service—the stoker, a rating introduced in 1826. His pay was 46 shillings (£2.30) a month, later increased to 54 shillings (£2.70). For many years the stoker was looked down upon by officers and seamen alike as an inferior.

The Navy, like the country in general, showed itself deeply conservative over the use of iron ships. The engineer Brunel laid down the first big iron ship, the *Great Britain*, in 1838. The Admiralty ordered a small flotilla of iron frigates only five years later, but such was the prejudice against them that they were degraded to act as troop-carriers. The triumph of iron, however, when it did come, was sudden and complete. The French launched a very large frigate, built of wood

37 Jackie Fisher (Admiral Lord Fisher)
See page **64**

but protected by iron plating, in 1859. Our reply was the *Warrior*, launched the following year, a much more revolutionary ship, with a hull built completely of iron. After that all new British warships were made of iron, and later steel; the best of the old wooden ones were adapted as far as possible above the water-line.

Gunnery

Naval gunnery had changed little during the three preceding centuries. In Nelson's ships the guns were loaded down the muzzle, the inside of the barrel was smooth, and they fired solid round, iron shot. This was all very well in Nelson's kind of action, when ships opened fire at very close range, but that era ended at Navarino. Curiously enough, explosive shells had been used with great effect by Sir Samuel Bentham in 1788, but as he was serving in the Russian Navy at the time, the Admiralty took no notice. In the 1820s a French general called Paixhans wrote two books in which he suggested scrapping the entire French Navy and replacing it with a fleet of paddle-steamers armed with guns firing explosive shells. With these, he claimed, his country could take its revenge for Trafalgar and finish Britain as a naval power for ever. Paixhans' ideas were not followed up, one reason being that shell-fire was considered too inhumane—a sobering thought in an age which has seen ever more horrible weapons designed and used with few protests about their inhumanity.

By 1864 a breech-loading rifle, firing an elongated bullet from a grooved barrel, was in general use in the British Army, and the development of naval guns followed the same course. Moored mines, intended to blow up enemy vessels, were first used by the Russians in the Crimean war; the torpedo was also a nineteenth-century invention, a primitive version being used in the American Civil War in the 1860s.

The development of submarines also dates from this period. There had been many attempts to design an underwater vessel from the time of Leonardo da Vinci onwards, but the first successful one was built in 1877 to the design of an Englishman, J. P. Holland. A great deal of research followed in a number of countries, side by side with the development of the torpedo. By 1914 the torpedo-carrying submarine was sufficiently developed to play an important part in the Great War.

It is perhaps surprising that new methods of ship construction and new weapons were adopted at all during this period, as the Navy was run by elderly officers determined to resist change whenever possible. Admiral Sir Edward Harvey, who had served in the battle of the Glorious First of June, became Commander-in-Chief at the Nore when well over 70; Sir William Bowles, a contemporary of Nelson, was appointed to the Portsmouth command at the age of 79.

New prospects for seamen

However, changes did come throughout the nineteenth century, and not only in ships and weapons. The admiralty set up a Commission on Manning, and its

38 The bombardment of the Turkish forts in the Dardanelles, 1915; a painting by Norman Wilkinson. *See page* **66**

report in 1853 made recommendations which marked the beginnings of a career structure for the men, in place of the old system of signing on a ship's crew for one commission and then discharging them. Men and boys were now to be taken on for ten years continuous service from the age of 18, and then placed on reserve, to be recalled if necessary up to the age of 48. Nevertheless, when the Crimean War broke out in 1854, it proved as difficult as ever to get men to volunteer for the Navy. Once in, however, they fought no less bravely than the men of Trafalgar. Although there were actions in the Arctic, the Far East and the Baltic, the Navy's greatest renown was won on land in the Crimea itself. A Naval Brigade with ship's guns ashore took part in much of the fighting, alongside the soldiers, and no less than ten sailors won the Victoria Cross (recently created as an award for the highest bravery).

After the war, it was obvious that the recent reforms had not gone far enough. A Royal Commission was set up in 1858 to make a thorough study of manning problems. Its recommendations covered terms of active and reserve service, pay, clothing and victuals and the training of boys and men.

The idea of continuous service was carried much further, with a first term of twelve years, followed, if a man volunteered to stay on, by ten years and then by further spells of five. A pension was payable after 22 years and increased for every five after that. If under 18, the recruit joined as a boy, if over that age as an ordinary seaman (at 38s 9d [£1.94] a month). Promotion to able seaman meant an increase of pay to 49s 1d (£2.45). There were now various ways of earning extra pay, such as the good conduct badge, worth 3d (1½p) per day; a man who did not draw his rum ration could take 7s 6d (37½p) a month instead. Proficiency in gunnery, torpedoes, signalling and so on now entitled a man to additional pay.

The nineteenth-century seaman, with career prospects, better pay and better food, also had better clothes. In 1857 a standard uniform was introduced for the first time—blue cloth jacket, blue trousers, white duck trousers, blue serge frock, white drill frock, square blue collar with the famous three rows of white tape, pea jacket, black silk scarf, black canvas hat with ribbon bearing the ship's name, a working hat without a peak, and a wide-brimmed straw hat. The canvas hat

39 Admiral Jellicoe, who commanded the Grand Fleet at the Battle of Jutland

and blue jacket were abolished, as later was the straw hat, but otherwise the uniform was very much as worn in modern times.

Punishment was gradually becoming less savage, though it was not until 1879 that flogging was officially forbidden. Lack of shore leave had always been a grievance, the traditional attitude being that if men were allowed ashore they would desert. In 1890 leave became a right rather than a privilege and all captains were required to grant it when the needs of the service allowed. Sailors' hostels were opened in seaports, notably by Miss Agnes Weston, who devoted her life to encouraging temperance and Christian behaviour on the lower deck.

After the Royal Commission of 1858, training was taken much more seriously. There were already several ships used for the training of boys, but now their number was increased by four large vessels, and all boys were given a period of training before being sent to join the fleet. The pay of naval school-masters was increased in order to attract better qualified teachers and boys were taught general subjects in addition to their nautical training. HMS *Excellent*, the famous gunnery school at Portsmouth (founded in 1830) was greatly enlarged and equipped to train larger numbers of men. When the torpedo was recognised as an important new weapon, a torpedo training school was established.

Admiral Lord Fisher

Apart from its surveying and anti-slave trade activities, the nineteenth-century Navy had to guard 'the Empire on which the sun never sets', and in 1884 a leading Liberal journalist, W. T. Stead, pointed out in a series of articles its inadequacy for carrying out this tremendous task. He showed that during the previous twenty years the other naval powers had increased their expenditure by 40 per cent, while Britain's naval budget had remained the same. Britain was trying to protect more widespread and vastly increased territories with completely inadequate resources. Stead's articles aroused immediate attention and an increased naval budget was rushed through Parliament.

Stead had obtained much of his information from a certain Captain Fisher, who was to play an important part in reforming the Navy. When he was made Commander-in-Chief of the Mediterranean Fleet, he increased shore leave, encouraged outdoor sports and improved the food rations. His next post was in charge of personnel and training, and before long he had introduced a new scheme for the training of officers, founded new schools ashore for boys, with an improved curriculum, and started the building of barracks at Chatham, Portsmouth and Devonport.

On promotion to First Sea Lord in 1904, 'Jackie' Fisher, as he was always called in the Navy, introduced a new type of battleship and battle-cruiser, big ships with big guns. They also had spacious messdecks, good bathrooms and wash-places, canteens and bakeries.

Fisher was certain that there would be war with Germany, sooner or later, and he deliberately concentrated as many ships as possible in home waters. Thus, when war did come in 1914, four years after Fisher's retirement, the Navy was reasonably well prepared. On their part, the Germans had not been idle; since the launching of Fisher's first new ship, the *Dreadnought*, in 1905, they had been building warships at a great rate.

Outbreak of the First World War

In 1914 everyone expected the war to begin with a battle between the two great Navies, but this was not to happen yet. The British fleet remained in its inhospitable anchorage at Scapa Flow in the Orkneys, with the destroyers at Harwich and a force at Dover (the famous Dover Patrol) to guard the Channel. It was the destroyers, backed up by submarines, which broke into the Bight of Heligoland in August 1914 and attacked the German fleet. The destroyers had the support of light cruisers and more important, the huge battle-cruisers under Admiral Beatty. It was Beatty's guns which won the day, for three German cruisers and a destroyer were sunk, and three more cruisers badly damaged.

The battle of Heligoland made the Germans more reluctant than before to risk a full-scale battle, and they concentrated on mine-laying and on the effort of their submarines, but without great effect. There could hardly be a greater contrast between wooden ships fighting it out at close quarters and armour-plated vessels opening fire at a range of several miles, but as in Nelson's day, power and accuracy with guns were of the first importance.

This was clearly shown in November 1914, when Admiral von Spee's best cruisers, *Scharnhorst* and *Greisenau*, armed with 9-inch (22.5-centimetre) guns, soon broke up a British squadron armed with 6-inch (15-centimetre) guns, off Coronel, on the Chilean coast. Lord Fisher, who had been recalled as First Sea Lord decided on revenge and sent the 12-inch (30-centimetre) gun battle-cruisers *Invincible* and *Inflexible* after the Germans. Once again heavier guns won the day, and the Germans were utterly defeated in the battle of the Falkland Islands.

The German battle-cruisers made several raids on British east coast towns. They escaped after heavily bombarding Yarmouth and Scarborough, but in January 1915 they were caught off the Dogger Bank between Admiral Jellicoe's force and that of Admiral Beatty. One German ship was sunk and several others set on fire, while Beatty's flagship, the *Lion*, was badly damaged. After this, the Germans gave up their raids for the time being and concentrated on submarine warfare, sinking British merchant ships wherever they could find them.

40 Admiral Beatty, who was in command of the battle-cruisers at Jutland

The Dardanelles

The year 1915 is remembered for the disastrous campaign in the Dardanelles, the straits at the entrance to the Sea of Marmora. Our Russian allies were in danger of complete defeat by the German armies, and Turkey's entry into the war on Germany's side made their situation even more desperate. In an attempt to help the Russians, British and French ships were sent to bombard the forts in the Dardanelles. After three ships had been sunk and three more damaged, mostly by mines, it was decided to attempt a landing. For eight months British, Australian, New Zealand and French troops, plus a Royal Naval Division, held on precariously in the Gallipoli peninsula. At the end of the year, when the operation had cost more than 250,000 casualties, an evacuation was ordered and the Navy took off the survivors. This severe defeat led to the collapse of one of our allies, Serbia, and the decision of Bulgaria to come in on the side of the Germans.

The Battle of Jutland

It was not until 1916 that the long-awaited major battle took place. On 31 May, in unusually misty weather, Beatty's battle-cruisers made contact with those of the Germans under Admiral Hipper. The main British fleet under Jellicoe came up at full speed and at last the two great Navies confronted one another. The British, with 28 battleships against 22, 9 battle-cruisers to 5, and more than twice as many cruisers as the enemy, were expecting a decisive victory. In the event, neither side really won the Battle of Jutland, the only large-scale naval action of the war. The British lost more ships and more men, but the German High Seas fleet never again risked a major engagement. At any rate they could take some satisfaction in having, with their new and relatively inexperienced Navy, taken on the greatest sea-power in the world. As far as the British fleet was concerned,

41 The Battle of Jutland: the British Grand Fleet in the North Sea

42 One of Britain's early submarines, first built in 1908, with twin screws and diesel engines

Jutland showed up several very serious weaknesses. Three battle-cruisers blew up because their shell magazines were not flash-proof and so could be exploded by an odd spark; decks were not sufficiently armour-plated to resist dropping shellfire, a German speciality; and British shells lacked penetrating and explosive power.

Submarine warfare

Once again the Germans relied on the ability of their submarines to sink merchant ships bringing food and supplies to Britain. This was against international law, which permitted only the confiscation of merchantmen in such circumstances. The greatly improved German submarines (U-boats) were so successful in their inhuman task that at one point Britain had only six weeks' supply of food left. Neutral ships, including those of the United States, were being lost, and the Germans knew that sooner or later the Americans would come into the war against them. Nevertheless, in February 1917, Germany announced a policy of unrestricted U-boat warfare, which meant that all merchant ships would be sunk at sight. For the United States this was intolerable and they declared war on 6 April. In February and March the U-boats had sunk well over one million tons of shipping; only a tremendous effort by British farmers saved the country from starvation.

American money and materials, the American fleet, and finally a large and well-equipped American army in France, had a decisive effect on the war. At last the Admiralty introduced the convoy system, by which destroyers accompanied groups of merchant ships instead of letting them sail alone and unprotected. The American shipyards were busy, and by the spring of 1918 merchant ships were being built faster than the U-boats could destroy them.

The German base for building submarines was Bruges, in Belgium, whence they were sent by canal to the North Sea at Ostend and Zeebrugge. On St George's Day, 23 April 1918, a special force under Admiral Sir Roger Keyes made a daring and successful attack on Zeebrugge, though attempts to block Ostend were a failure. However, the U-boat menace was now over, and the end of the war not far off. The German people, nearly starved by the British blockade, were in a revolutionary mood, and heartily sick of the war. The German fleet had been too long in harbour, and its morale was desperately low. The sailors, like the

43 The end of the German High Seas Fleet. The *Hindenburg* after scuttling at Scapa Flow, 1919

civilians, were affected by the ideas of the Communist Revolution in Russia, and in October 1918, when ordered to sea, the High Seas Fleet hoisted the Red Flag and mutinied. The war ended on 11 November, and ten days later the German fleet surrendered. The larger ships were interned at Scapa Flow, with German caretaker crews aboard under the command of Admiral von Reuter. In June 1919 von Reuter gave secret orders for the ships to be scuttled, and before the British Navy could prevent it, nearly all the High Seas Fleet was beneath the waves.

The First World War was mainly fought on land and huge armies confronted one another in battles where many thousands of men were killed in a single day. All the same, the Navy played an important part by keeping the German fleet in harbour and blockading the supply routes.

In its composition it was a different kind of Navy from any that had preceded it. Its backbone was the professional sailor, but its numbers were augmented by a great many volunteers, and during the second half of the war, by conscripts. Both the 'regulars' and the 'Hostilities Only' temporaries learned a great deal from one another. Those who had spent most of their lives in the service were sometimes surprised to find that civilians, once aboard a ship, could be good messmates and after a time, quite useful seaman, while those who had joined for 'Hostilities Only' often came to like and respect the professionals. A. Trystan Edwards spent most of the war as a seaman after a public school and university education. In his book *Three Rows of Tape* (published by Heinemann), he wrote:

Besides the sociability and complete lack of self-consciousness which are induced by life on the Lower Deck, we here encounter a quality of manliness not so easily acquired in the great Public Schools, for life aboard ship is more severe and the young sailor has the additional advantage of sharing serious responsibilities with other men. When once this habit of sociability has been established . . . it becomes a second nature to such an extent that the bluejacket spontaneously extends to others outside his circle the same friendliness and open-heartedness that have been acquired within it.

6 The Second World War

The inter-war years
We have already seen how the end of each major war brought about a drastic reduction in the size of our Navy. The years following 1918 were no exception, though there were several new circumstances. The principal one was an effort among the great powers to reach agreement on limiting the size of their fleets. A series of conferences was held, at the first of which, in 1921, Britain was allowed equality in naval strength with the USA, Japan 40 per cent less, and France and Italy still smaller percentages. This meant the end of our supremacy at sea; henceforth Britannia did not rule the waves, but only some of them. At the third conference, in 1930, Britain, the USA and Japan agreed not to replace capital ships for 6 years or to build new ones for 15, but France and Italy were under no such restriction.

After the war, Sir Eric Geddes had given the job of devising economies in the Navy, and the 'Geddes Axe' was responsible for the compulsory retirement of more than 1,200 junior officers on very small pensions. During the period covered by the conferences, the Navy's budget had been steadily lowered until in 1932 it was only £50½ million.

In 1931, at a time of world-wide trade depression, when Britain had an unemployment rate of about 20 per cent, the Admiralty decided on a pay cut for the Navy. The news only reached the fleet at Invergordon after the men had heard it on the radio and read it in the newspapers. The cut which was the most bitterly resented was the reduction of an able seaman's pay from 4s (20p) to 3s (15p) a day. Protest meetings were held and the fleet did something it had never done before—it actually went on strike. The battleships *Rodney* and *Valiant* were due to sail for exercises, but the crews refused. Work was stopped in all the other ships and the strikers sent a petition to the Admiralty asking for a revision of the pay cuts. These were in fact reduced to 10 per cent, but in spite of the official policy of 'no victimisation', the leaders were marked down and eventually dismissed.

In 1935–1936 a fourth Naval Conference was held in London, and after a great deal of argument, some agreement was reached about the maximum size permitted for future ships. The ratio system was abandoned, and Britain was thus able to start rebuilding what had become an almost non-existent Navy. Between 1933 and 1938, 7 battleships, 13 cruisers, 5 aircraft carriers and 15 destroyers were laid down or authorised. During these years international tension mounted—in Europe two dictators, Adolf Hitler in Germany and Benito Mussolini in Italy,

44 The Graf Spee: Battle of the River Plate, 1939

were becoming ever more grandiose in their ambitions, while in the Far East Japan's attack on China marked the beginning of her aggressive policy.

The threat from Germany

The principal menace to Britain was Adolf Hitler, but it was not until after he had annexed Austria and Czechoslovakia and, in 1939, marched into Poland that we declared war. In the period since 1918 there had been several developments which greatly affected sea warfare, the most important being the improved aeroplane, which made reconnaissance infinitely more efficient. Before the Battle of Jutland, one British seaplane flew briefly over the German fleet, but only after it had been spotted from the surface. In the 1939 war, as we shall see, aircraft played a tremendously important part over land and sea. Parallel with the development of aircraft was that of the bomb and the torpedo, both of which could now be airborne. Something entirely new was direction-finding, although crude devices for detecting submarines had been used during the U-boat crisis of 1917. Intensive research led to the development of a truly revolutionary invention called radar during the later stages of the 1939 war.

The Germans had been planning an immense expansion of their Navy, but at the outbreak of war in September 1939 it had hardly started. The only big ships in commission were three so-called pocket battleships, two normal battleships (*Scharnhorst* and *Greisenau*) and one cruiser. The pocket battleships, designed as long distance raiders, were fast, heavily armour-plated and carrying six 11-inch (28-centimetre) guns.

Soon after the beginning of the war, one of these, the *Graf Spee*, was successfully operating against merchant shipping in the South Atlantic. Her captain became over-bold and left the open seas for the mouth of the River Plate, between Uruguay and Argentina. Here he was caught by the British cruisers *Exeter* and *Ajax*, and

Achilles of the New Zealand Navy. The German ship had the advantage of radar and she soon damaged all three cruisers, but after being hit more than 20 times, she made for the neutral port of Montevideo. *Ajax* and *Achilles*, with *Cumberland* replacing the badly damaged *Exeter*, watched the estuary for some days, until *Graf Spee* left harbour and scuttled herself.

The 'phoney' war
The first winter of the war became known as the 'phoney war'; the expected air raids on British cities did not happen, and on the Continent, German and allied armies faced one another from supposedly impregnable positions. At sea, however, it was a real war, with British warships and merchantmen under attack from mines, torpedoes and bombs. In the first month a U-boat sank the aircraft carrier *Courageous* to the west of Ireland; in October the famous German submariner Günther Prien made a daring raid into Scapa Flow and sank the battleship *Royal Oak*. One hundred and sixty-four of our merchant ships were lost in the first six months, and the number would probably have been much higher if Hitler's concentration on overrunning Europe had not made him refuse to speed up the construction of U-boats.

Norway
In 1940 both sides had plans to occupy neutral Norway, but the Germans acted first, in early April, landing at a number of places between Oslo and Narvik, with strong naval support. All our available ships were sent northwards and some successful attacks were made on the invasion areas. One German cruiser was sunk by aircraft and another by submarine, while the pocket battleship *Lützow* was put out of action for a year. As for the enemy destroyers, a number were sunk or damaged, and the rest were finished off in an attempt to recapture Narvik.

45 Günther Prien, the U-boat commander who sank the *Royal Oak* at Scapa Flow and was killed in action in 1941

The latter attack by the battleship *Warspite* and nine destroyers threw the Germans into complete confusion and gave us a base in Norway.

This did not last long: the German army was advancing northward, and an attempt to halt it by landing troops around Trondheim had to be given up and the troops taken off by British and French ships. In Narvik the demoralisation of the Germans and the loss of their destroyers was not followed up by a landing until it was too late. On 27 May, after the Germans had returned, British, French and Polish troops were put ashore, and by the following day had taken the town. The main German armies had by then defeated the Dutch and Belgians and were dashing across France towards the Channel. There was only one thing for the Allies to do—withdraw from Norway. The evacuation was carried out by passenger liners with a strong naval escort. The RAF fighters which had been operating in Norway were embarked in the aircraft carrier *Glorious*; escorted only by two destroyers, she was suddenly sighted by *Scharnhorst* and *Greisenau* and sunk without difficulty. In the evacuation three British ships and nearly 1500 men were lost—the final disaster in the calamitous Norwegian campaign. We could only have succeeded in Norway with strong air support, and this was something we were not to possess for several more years.

Evacuation of Dunkirk

A far bigger evacuation now faced the Navy, starting with the Dutch ports, bringing out merchant ships and embarking the Netherlands Royal family and Government under continuous air attack. A few days later the withdrawal of the British army from the French ports commenced. Over 4,000 soldiers were picked up from Boulogne just ahead of the German advance. For the main task at Dunkirk every available craft had been hastily assembled. Destroyers and cross-Channel steamers took the greatest number, but drifters, coasters, tugs and even

46   The evacuation from Dunkirk, 1940

47 The Italian battleship, *the Vittorio Veneto*

lifeboats were crammed with exhausted soldiers. By 4 June, over one-third of a million men had been rescued, including more than 26,000 French. Smaller operations went on from the other ports until the surrender of the French Government made it impossible to continue; in addition to those rescued at Dunkirk, nearly 200,000 were brought to England, among them French, Poles, Czechs and a few Belgians.

Britain was now completely isolated from Europe, and it might have been expected that Hitler's next step would be to invade. Plans were actually made for a main landing between Beachy Head and Folkestone, with another between Selsey Bill and Brighton. Transport ships, lighters and barges, motor boats and other craft were hastily assembled at various ports, and as a preliminary the German Air Force started massive bombing raids on British towns and cities.

Fear of invasion

Why then did the invasion never take place? There were various reasons; disagreements between the German army and Navy led to postponement from August 1940 to September, and in October it was decided to put it off until the following spring or summer. Unsettled weather was another factor, added to which the Germans had an exaggerated idea of our anti-invasion preparations. Naval and RAF aircraft carried out some very effective bombing of the invasion ports, while our fighters shot down great numbers of German bombers during the Battle of Britain.

48 The aircraft carrier *Ark Royal* sinking after being torpedoed in the Mediterranean, 1941. Swordfish aircraft are still on the flight deck

Hitler had not achieved the air supremacy which might have made up for lack of sea power by keeping our Navy out of the invasion area. The German Admiral Ruge summed up the position in a book he wrote some time after the war; 'Had Hitler been able to dominate the English Channel—be it only for 24 hours—he might have succeeded. But like Napoleon before him, he was never in a position to do so'.

Control of the seas was now essential for our survival. Convoys had to be protected and we were desperately short of escort craft. The celebrated 'Flower class' corvettes were at sea in numbers in May 1940, but as they had been originally designed for coastal duties, they had to be modified before they could become the mainstay of our convey escorts. Frigates, designed for ocean work, were not ready for sea until 1942. As far as air escort was concerned, Coastal Command had no aircraft or crews available at the outbreak of war. The Fleet Air Arm was not started until 5 months later, so there was much lost time to be made up in naval aviation. Many Fleet Air Arm pilots were flying obsolete wooden aircraft called Swordfish, which remained operational throughout the war.

Italy enters the war

Italy came into the war on the German side in the eventful month of June 1940 and greatly altered our position in the Mediterranean. Our fleet there was greatly outnumbered by the large Italian Navy; our vital base at Malta was vulnerable to air attack, and we had too few submarines.

It was this weak position which led to one of our most regrettable actions of the war. Part of the French fleet had gone to Oran, in Algeria, after the surrender. In July 1940, after they had been given an ultimatum to join us or proceed to a British or a French West Indian port, the French ships were attacked by a British force from Gibraltar. Two battleships were wrecked, one cruiser beached and another damaged; this last ship, accompanied by the destroyers, escaped to

Toulon. Other French warships at Alexandria and in British ports were seized and their crews disarmed. In September an attack was made on French ships at Dakar, their main West Africa base. A Free French headquarters had now been set up in London under General de Gaulle, and he was convinced that he would be immediately welcomed in Dakar. This proved not to be the case, and the affair was an inglorious failure, with damage to the battleship *Resolution* and four other vessels, and much ill-feeling among the French, as the only results.

The Italians showed little inclination to fight our Mediterranean fleet. They had missed their chance by November 1940, when their base at Taranto was attacked by Swordfish aircraft from the *Illustrious*. Two cruisers and three of Italy's five battleships were severely damaged for the loss of two Swordfish. This brilliant action gave us naval superiority in the Mediterranean and enabled us to continue sending supplies to Greece. Greece had been suddenly invaded by the Italians in October, but they were putting up a good fight. The island of Crete was soon afterwards occupied by British troops as a useful half-way point between Malta and Alexandria. These bases had to be kept supplied by convoy via Gibraltar and at this time the Italian Air Force was too occupied in Greece to do much against them.

German forces in the Mediterranean
This situation was changed by the arrival of a powerful and well-trained German force of about 300 aircraft in Sicily. These made their first attack in January 1941 on a large and heavily-escorted Malta convoy. By accurate dive-bombing the

49 A British destroyer in heavy seas

50 The Flower class corvette *Hibiscus*, one of the hard-working convoy escorts during the battle of the Atlantic

Stukas, as they were called, damaged the aircraft carrier *Illustrious* and two cruisers.

At that time Malta, with inadequate anti-aircraft defences and too few fighter planes, was a sitting target for the Germans, and was continuously bombed during the next few months. Fortunately, however, Hitler's Italian allies were being driven back in North Africa, and to help them he transferred nearly half his air force from Sicily, so the attacks on Malta became less fierce. German troops, the famous Afrika Korps, were also sent out to reinforce the retreating Italians. Pressure was put on the Italian Navy to put to sea and attack our convoys, and at the end of March Admiral Cunningham's Eastern Mediterranean fleet made contact with them off Cape Matapan, to the south of Greece. One Italian cruiser was disabled by air attack, and while searching for her, two others were blown up, as well as two destroyers. The disabled cruiser was then sunk; no British ships were lost in the action, in which victory resulted from efficient use of aircraft and accurate gunnery.

The Italians were proving to be a liability to Hitler, and once again, this time in Greece, he took over from their unsuccessful forces. His armies invaded in April 1941 and rapidly overran the country. After the Greek surrender, British troops had to be got out: this was done at night, to avoid enemy bombers, and nearly all the troops were rescued, with only the loss of 2 destroyers and 2 troop-carriers. Next month came the German airborne invasion of Crete, and once again the Navy had to take off our soldiers, this time with heavy loss of ships.

The loss of Crete made the defence of Malta absolutely vital. Two more convoys got through in 1941, in spite of massive attacks by German aircraft, acting on Hitler's special order to stop supplies at any price. They were very costly operations in terms of losses and damage among the escorting warships.

We now had more aircraft based on the island, and both they and the Malta submarine flotilla had much success in attacking enemy convoys bound for North Africa. In November they sank about 70 per cent of the cargoes, a serious setback to the heavily-mechanised Afrika Korps, dependent on supplies of fuel for its armoured vehicles. To cope with this situation, Hitler ordered U-boats into the

Mediterranean, and they had two quick and notable successes, destroying our only available modern aircraft carrier, *Ark Royal*, and the battleship *Barham*. Soon afterwards Italian midget submarines made a daring attack on our ships in Alexandria harbour and crippled the battleships *Valiant* and *Queen Elizabeth*.

The Far East
The black year of 1941 ended with the lightning attack by Japanese carrier-borne bombers on the American fleet at Pearl Harbour, Hawaii. All the eight battleships were disabled and numerous other ships damaged. Three days later, Japanese bombers sank our *Prince of Wales* and *Repulse* and were soon to start their swift advance through South-East Asia. The war had now spread throughout the world, with the United States and Russia (attacked by Hitler in June 1941) on our side, and Japan as a powerful ally of Germany and Italy.

Convoys to Russia
Hitler's invasion of Russia meant a lessening of German efforts in the Mediterranean as resources were concentrated on the eastern front. It also meant that our Navy, already stretched to the utmost, had to take on another dangerous task. Russia desperately needed help, and the only help we were able to give was in the form of supplies, especially tanks and guns. These had to be sent to Russia's northern ports round the tip of Norway, past a long strip of enemy-held coastline. There was danger of attack from Norwegian airfields, from U-boats and from the biggest ships of the German fleet, now based in Norway. At first the convoys reached port unharmed, though one of them, escorted only by two corvettes and two minesweepers, had a narrow escape from meeting the battleship *Tirpitz* and some destroyers. As time went on, however, losses mounted, until the disaster of PQ17, the code number for the seventeenth convoy to Russia. This consisted of

51 The little ships of the Coastal Forces on patrol. These small craft, mostly manned by Hostilities Only sailors, saw plenty of action in various parts of the world between 1939 and 1945

35 merchantmen, more than half of them American, and a very large naval force, including battleships and cruisers. Several determined air attacks had been fought off without much loss, when the Admiralty, far away from the scene of action, sent a signal for the cruisers to 'withdraw to westward at high speed'. This was followed by another ordering the convoy to 'disperse and proceed to Russian ports'—and yet another ordering it to 'scatter'. The eventual result was that only one-third of the merchant ships reached harbour. The next convoy, also strongly escorted, fought off attacks by German torpedo bombers, shot down more than 40 of them, and reached Russia with the loss of one-third of the freighters. There is no doubt that manning these Arctic convoys was the most dangerous job of the whole war. To the certainty of fierce attacks and long spells at 'action stations' in the world's worst weather was added the chance of freezing to death in the icy waters.

The Atlantic
The Battle of the Atlantic continued its long drawn out course. 1941 had seen plenty of activity, with the U-boats starting to operate in packs from the spring onwards. After Germany declared war on the United States in December, U-boats were at once sent to American east coastal waters. They took full advantage of the United States' lack of anti-submarine forces and in January 1942 they sank 40 ships in less than 3 weeks. The introduction of convoys in American waters gradually reduced the rate of loss and by July the worst was over. Better radar and improved depth charges were making life more difficult for the U-boats, though they were now operating in a far wider area than ever before—the Caribbean, off South America, West Africa and the Cape of Good Hope. When the convoy system in United States coastal waters reduced their effectiveness there, more were available for attacks on North Atlantic convoys. In the second half of 1942 and on into 1943, we were losing supply ships at an alarming rate, sometimes over 100 a month.

The Pacific
In the Pacific, the Japanese continued to make full use of their sea-power. In the Battle of the Java Sea and other engagements in February and March 1942, they sank six cruisers, one American, two Dutch, one British and two Australian. They then invaded the Dutch colonies of Java, Borneo and Sumatra, landed in New Guinea, and bombed Australia's northern bases. These lightning advances were not continued; at one time it looked as if the Japanese would attack Ceylon, but this never happened. The United States Navy was mustering in increasing strength in the Pacific, and in May and June 1942, won two great victories in the battles of the Coral Sea and Midway Island. Although the war was to last three more years, these battles should be remembered as the beginning of the road to final victory.

52 Supplies for Malta: the fast minelayer *Welshman* arrives in the Grand Harbour

British Coastal Forces

Around our own coasts as well as in the Mediterranean the increasing numbers of small ships of Coastal Forces—motor gunboats, torpedo boats, launches—had been continuously busy, escorting convoys, attacking enemy shipping, engaging their German opposite numbers (known as E-boats) and so on. They also took part in raids on the coast of Europe by Combined Operations, a force including Marine Commandos set up for that purpose. In March 1942 the ex-American destroyer *Campbeltown* and seventeen Coastal Forces craft sailed up the river Loire to St Nazaire. Their object was to destroy the entrance lock to the harbour, which was the only one on the French Atlantic coast big enough to hold the *Tirpitz*, and also to do as much damage as possible to one of Germany's most important bases for the battle of the Atlantic. *Campbeltown* was to ram the lock gates and then be blown up after the Commandos had demolished as much as they could of the port installations. The raid succeeded, but the cost was heavy; all the Marines were killed or captured and only three of the Coastal Forces vessels reached their home port. A daylight raid on Dieppe in August, with Canadian infantry as well as a Marine Commando, was beaten off with heavy losses. However, useful experience had been gained on the technique of amphibious attack.

The Mediterranean, 1942

In the Mediterranean, things went badly during the early months of 1942. The brilliant German general Rommel had thrust eastwards and in July was only 60 miles (96 kilometres) from Alexandria, ready to press on to Cairo and the Red Sea. He was halted by the British Eighth Army at El Alamein, and later defeated and driven back in the battle of that name. The situation on Malta had become

53 (*left*) A U-boat torpedoes a British merchant ship

54 (*above*) The Navy's revenge: one of the former American destroyers at the destruction of a U-boat

desperate by March, after a convoy had been forced to turn back in the previous month. Four supply ships from Alexandria, heavily escorted, met a powerful Italian force, and after beating them off was fiercely attacked by German bombers. Two of the merchant ships were lost, but the others, although damaged, reached Malta and were unloaded in spite of further bombardment. Additional fighter planes reached the island and in May the fast minelayer *Welshman* got through, laden with much-needed ammunition.

In June the situation was again very serious and simultaneous convoys set out from Alexandria and Gibraltar. The westward convoy had to turn back, after three destroyers had been lost and three cruisers damaged, but the one from Gibraltar, with battleship, aircraft carrier and cruiser escort, got two of its five ships through to Malta. In August another attempt was made from Gibraltar, with a huge naval escort—two battleships, four aircraft carriers, seven cruisers and 25 destroyers! After the loss of the carrier *Eagle*, two cruisers and a destroyer, five of the supply ships reached port and Malta was saved. By September air attacks on the island had diminished so much that it was possible for some of the cruisers and destroyers to be used for attacking enemy supply lines in the Mediterranean.

November saw British and American forces landing at several points in North-West Africa. Except at Oran, the French garrisons did not resist very strongly, and the newly-landed forces were able to move eastward to link up with the Eighth Army and cut the enemy off in Tunisia. The Navy was kept busy supporting the land forces, delivering supplies and clearing harbours while continuing to help Malta. In spite of heavy air attacks, minesweepers were able to clear a channel from Tunis to Tripoli, so that a convoy from Gibraltar reached Alexandria safely in May 1943. The whole Mediterranean was now open for the first time since Italy came into the war.

The next step was the invasion of Sicily in July, again carried out by a huge Anglo-American force with complete surprise. The island was in Allied hands a few weeks later, though the enemy forces had time to escape across the Messina Straits to Italy.

Landing on the Italian mainland was the obvious follow-up to this success, and Salerno, south of Naples, was the place chosen. The Italians surrendered in September and their fleet, except one battleship sunk by the Germans on the way, reached Malta just after the Salerno landings began. Although one enemy was out of the way, the invading troops met tough resistance from first-class German soldiers, who at one point forced their way between the British and Americans. Tremendous bombardment from the sea and air had their effect, and the allied forces were able to advance. A further landing in January 1944 at Anzio, south of Rome, was also strongly resisted, and it was not until May that a real break-through was made.

Russian convoys are resumed

Meanwhile, the Navy's other main tasks continued—the Battle of the Atlantic and the Russian convoys (resumed in December 1942). In that month five British destroyers held up a much more powerful German force to protect a convoy to Russia. The German ships, which included a pocket battleship, were then driven off by the cruisers *Jamaica* and *Sheffield*; when Hitler heard the news, he screamed with rage for hours. Two more convoys got through, but in spring 1943, air reconnaissance showed that three German battleships were at Alten Fjord, on the north coast of Norway. As it was impossible to protect convoys against these, they had to stop and every available escort ship was used in the Atlantic.

There the convoys were already being guarded more strongly, with auxiliary carriers as well as long-range Liberator aircraft. Nevertheless, in the autumn of 1942, ships were still being sunk faster than they could be replaced. The German command, however, was taken by surprise by the supply and troop convoys bound for the North African landings, and these got through safely. U-boats were

55 The cruiser *Suffolk* in the Arctic. A gun's crew cleaning a pompom (a multi-barrelled anti-aircraft gun)

56 The deck of the corvette *Narcissus* in the north Atlantic

rushed to the Mediterranean but had little effect on the strongly escorted convoys there. In the Atlantic, sinkings decreased sharply after November 1942, the worst month of all. In the spring, well over 100 U-boats were operational and their last big success was in March when they sank 85 ships in convoy in the North Atlantic. After that, their efforts fell away, this time for good, as their own losses mounted steadily.

Germany suffers losses
In September 1943 there took place one of the most daring feats of the war, when British midget submarines (x-craft) made their way into Alten Fjord and placed two delayed-action charges under the hull of the *Tirpitz*, putting her out of action for 6 vital months. As the *Lützow* had returned to Germany for a refit, only *Scharnhorst* and a few destroyers were left in northern Norway. Arctic convoys could now be resumed, and in November and early December they were unmolested. On Christmas Day *Scharnhorst* and her destroyers put to sea to find a convoy known to be on the way to Russia. After two short actions with the cruiser escorts, who inflicted some damage, she made off at high speed. The battleship *Duke of York* intercepted her; *Scharnhorst*, the faster ship, would have escaped but for an attack by destroyers, in which she was damaged. The *Duke of York* and two cruisers were able to get within range and they gave her a terrible pounding. *Scharnhorst's* speed fell to barely 5 knots, and the magnificent ship was finally sunk by no less than 11 torpedoes from the destroyers. Of her crew of nearly 2,000, only 36 were picked up, many more having died in the bitterly cold and tempestuous sea. This entirely new type of action, fought at long range, at night and in very rough weather, would have been impossible without the recent great improvements in radar.

D-day

Six months later, on 6 June 1944, the greatest 'Combined Operation' of all time began. In extremely unpleasant weather, over 5,000 ships, from battleships to the tiny vessels of Coastal Forces, covered the disembarkation in Normandy of troops and weapons from over 4,000 landing craft. The preliminary work of bombardment and minesweeping was as always carried out by the Navy. One of the most remarkable feats was the transporting across the Channel of two prefabricated 'Mulberry' harbours, more than $1\frac{1}{2}$ million tons of material. By the end of 'D-day', a beach-head 50 miles (80 kilometres) long had been established and the leading troops were fighting their way inland.

57 Tank landing ship on the way to the Normandy beaches

58 One of the invasion beaches, Normandy, 1944

The next few months were a particularly busy time for the Navy's small craft. They were constantly at sea, defending the essential supply lines to Normandy, not only against E-boats, but midget submarines and a new weapon, the explosive motorboat. U-boats caused little trouble, as only a small number managed to reach the invasion area. Fortunately, the greatly improved type developed by the Germans only came into operation just before the end of the war, and then only in small numbers.

The end of the war

American troops landed in the south of France in August, practically unopposed, and within two weeks the ports of Toulon and Marseilles were in their hands. During the closing months of the war most of Germany's surviving big ships were sunk in harbour by British or American bombers, so that only two cruisers remained when the surrender came in May 1945.

All that now remained to be done was to defeat the Japanese. In the Pacific the Americans had been on the offensive for some time, recapturing one by one the islands taken during the first victorious advance of the Japanese. The British Navy was now free to give more help in the Far East, and by the beginning of April 1945 many of our most powerful ships were assembled at the Australian port of Sydney. By that time, however, the Americans were already occupying Okinawa Island, only 350 miles (560 kilometres) from the mainland of Japan, and our fleet was only in time to take part in the bombing and minelaying operations before the Japanese surrender in August 1945.

59   Midget submarine: craft of this type were used by both sides in the Second World War

7 The Navy in the Nuclear Age

At the end of the war there were 790,000 officers and men and 74,000 women serving in the British Navy. They were a complete cross-section of the population, for the 'Hostilities Only' personnel greatly outnumbered the professional sailors. One could find a farm pupil becoming an expert gunner, a journalist the coxswain of a motor torpedo boat, a bank clerk commanding a minesweeper, and even an artist as a gunnery instructor. They could not fail to return to civilian life with their mental horizons immensely widened.

In 1945 we had more ships than ever before—14 battleships, 52 aircraft carriers, 62 cruisers, 257 destroyers, 131 submarines and nearly 9,000 smaller craft from frigates downward. Of these, only the minesweepers had an immediate job to do, in clearing the many minefields laid by both sides. Of the rest, many were paid off, disposed of to Commonwealth or other navies, or sold for scrap.

Modernisation of ships

Modernisation of the remaining ships was an obvious necessity, as composition of the fleet would have to be very different in the future. As we have seen, the day of the battleship was well and truly over; during the war its place as a main weapon of attack had been taken by the aircraft carrier. In 1945 a naval pilot made the world's first deck landing in a jet aircraft, and it was possible to start re-equipping the Fleet Air Arm with jet fighters and strike aircraft which could carry nuclear weapons. Carriers had to be modified for the handling of these faster and heavier machines, and several improvements were developed by the Navy, such as the angled deck to enable more aircraft to be operated at the same time, and the steam catapult for smoother and faster take-off.

Our last battleship was launched in 1944 and completed after the end of the war. She was the *Vanguard*, the largest warship ever built in Britain, and designed to be proof against any kind of attack. She remained in commission, an expensive and out-of-date relic, until the 1950s, when she was put into the reserve or 'mothball' fleet and finally sold for scrap in 1960.

In June 1953, the Coronation Review of the Fleet took place, when the Queen inspected the finest ships of the Navy, assembled at Spithead. *Vanguard* was the only battleship present, although four more, of the King George V class, were still in the reserve fleet. There were six British cruisers, as well as six from other countries, and numerous frigates and aircraft carriers. Prominent among these last was the *Eagle*, and the official programme of the Review made special

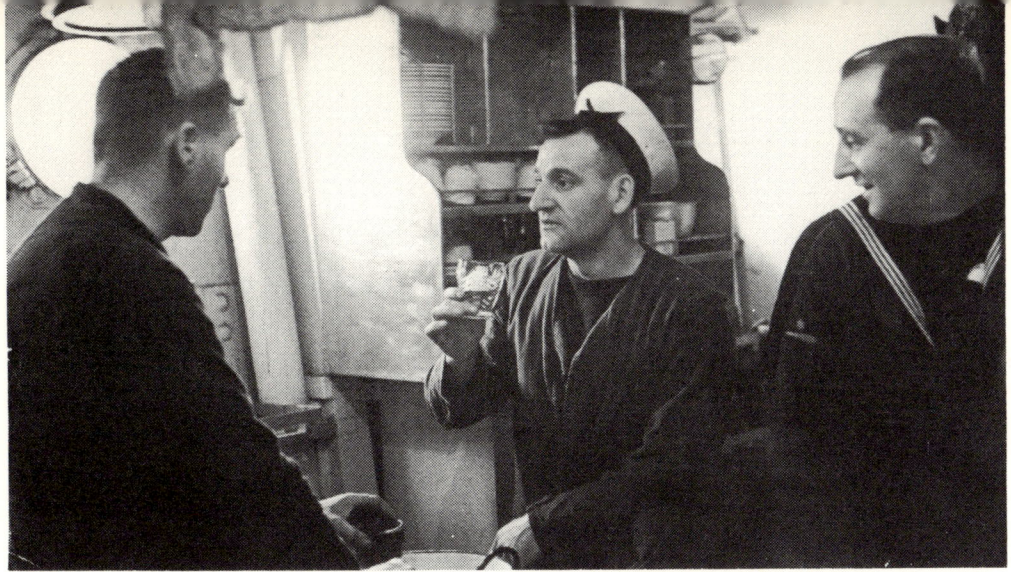

60 The rum ration, originally one pint (0.6 litres) per day per man, was reduced several times. In modern times is was $\frac{1}{8}$-pint, normally diluted with water. The rum ration was abolished in 1970

reference to the improvements in accommodation for the crew. 'The ship's company take their meals in two large dining halls. . . . Apart from the obvious advantages of this system, such as the fact that the meals are always served hot, it has the effect of removing all meals from the messdecks, so that these become in effect sleeping and recreation spaces. On his messdeck, each man has his own kit locker and another smaller one for his personal effects. The ship's company sleep in hammocks and many of the messdecks are air-conditioned'. This was a great advance on wartime conditions, and showed that although the increasingly complicated equipment demanded more space, better conditions for the crew were not being forgotten.

Although the battleship has gone, the cruiser still remains; where possible, these have been modernised and given radar-controlled quick-firing guns and automated remote-controlled machinery to make them faster. The Navy's increased use of large helicopters rendered some of the older cruisers obsolete, and those which could not be adapted were scrapped. Two of the more recently constructed were converted into helicopter carriers.

Another important type of ship in the modern Navy came into being in 1962: the guided-missile destroyer of nearly 6,000 tons. In spite of its name, this is a more powerful fighting ship than the old cruisers, armed with guided missiles as well as radar-controlled guns. A new development to give additional speed is the use of gas turbines to boost its steam turbine engines.

The place of the old-style destroyer has been taken by the frigate, built in large numbers since the war. Although only about 2,000 tons, these ships are powerfully armed and are capable of carrying a small landing party of Royal Marines if required.

61 HMS *Norfolk*, a guided-missile destroyer, completed 1970

Nuclear submarines

It is the submarine, however, which has undergone the most revolutionary change. Two years after the Coronation Review, a ship was sent to sea which was the first in the world to be powered by atomic energy. She was the submarine *Nautilus* of the United States Navy. In 1957 *Nautilus* visited Britain, and several Cabinet Ministers were among the visitors who went aboard. The Minister of Defence described his visit as 'an unforgettable experience', and went on to say, 'This nuclear submarine represents in the sphere of naval warfare a revolutionary advance as great as the change from sail to steam'.

The First Sea Lord, who was also present, was Lord Mountbatten, always noted for his forward-looking policies. Plans and drawings for a British nuclear submarine had already been prepared, and Lord Mountbatten saw to it that the project made good progress. Accordingly our first ship of this kind was launched in 1960 and named *Dreadnought* after Admiral Fisher's historic battleship of 1908. She is powered by a pressurised water-cooled reactor which gives an underwater speed of over 20 knots. Living conditions for the crew, always a problem in submarines, are far better than anything achieved in previous under-water vessels. Ships of this type are known as fleet submarines, and are mainly intended for defending lines of communication at sea against enemy submarines.

In 1967 the first of an even larger class of nuclear submarine was completed, this time armed with 16 Polaris missiles, which have an accurate range of 2,500 miles (4,000 kilometres), as well as homing torpedoes. These large ships of 7,500 tons, which can operate at sea anywhere in the world, can be looked upon as the battleships of the nuclear age.

Non-nuclear or 'conventional' submarines have undergone changes in design and their engines have been modified to make them faster and quieter. Complicated radar and interception devices have been developed and installed, and homing torpedoes are now their principal weapon. Like the nuclear submarines, they can operate equally well in the Arctic or the tropics.

Special-purpose ships

Mines were developed to a great extent during the war, and they can now be laid by aircraft, submarines or surface vessels. The modern Navy therefore has a large number of coastal and inshore minesweepers, designed to deal with any type of mine. These will eventually be replaced by Mine Countermeasures ships, which are now at the design stage.

Ships for amphibious landings are very different from the landing craft of D-day. In the early 1960s two assault ships were built, essentially a kind of floating dock for holding landing craft, which can be launched from the open stern. There is also space for vehicles, tanks and guns, a flight of assault helicopters and accommodation for a large landing force. The purpose of the assault ship is to carry everything needed for an amphibious operation and also to act as headquarters while it is being carried out. Another new type is the Commando ship, the first of which, a converted aircraft carrier, went into service in 1960. These ships carry a complete commando, about 700 officers and men, and in an emergency a second commando, as well as helicopters for landing them.

The idea behind the development of these two types of ship is that it is necessary now that we no longer have naval bases all over the world, to be able to mount a completely self-contained landing operation in case a limited war should break out or be threatened. On several occasions the commando ship has proved its worth. For example, in 1961, the ruler of Kuwait, in the Persian Gulf, asked for British help when in danger of aggression. A commando ship arrived within 24 hours and Marines were landed to guard Kuwait's borders. Army units arrived later and the threat of aggression was averted.

Non-military duties

Apart from duties of this kind, the Navy continues its unglamorous but useful

62 A modern engine room. Operating remote-controlled engines

63 A messdeck in the 1970s

tasks such as surveying and fishery protection. Since the days of Captain Cook it has always been to the fore in surveying the seas and coasts and preparing accurate charts, and with the help of modern techniques and methods, it does so today. As for fishery protection, this was very much in the news in 1972, after Iceland contravened an international agreement by which she could claim exclusive fishing rights within 12 miles (19 kilometres) of her own coasts. She increased the fishing limit to 50 miles (80 kilometres), and on 23 October 1972, the British Government stated that two frigates, *Achilles* and *Phoebe*, would be stationed just outside that limit to support British trawlers.

Policing the seas

In 1945, with 49 other states, Britain signed the charter of the United Nations, one of the main objects of which was the peaceful settlement of disputes. In 1949, the North Atlantic Treaty for mutual defence was signed by ourselves, the United States, France and various other western European countries. From time to time British ships have formed part of a force under the control of these organisations. In 1950, when the Communist armies of North Korea invaded the republic of South Korea, 34 of our ships took part in the United Nations operation against this aggression. As far as NATO is concerned, naval exercises are held from time to time, in which our ships are able to practise operating with those of our allies under a single command.

The modern seaman
The Royal Navy today consists of about 75,000 men and women, about one-tenth of the number at the end of the war. There are far fewer ships too, of course, but this small Navy is a modern, highly-mechanised and most efficient service. The British sailor today is trained to operate extremely complicated and expensive machinery and this calls for some qualities very different from those possessed by the simple, illiterate seamen of Nelson's day. There are other qualities which have not changed. In 1944, J. P. W. Mallalieu, formerly a journalist and now a Member of Parliament, wrote a book called *Very Ordinary Seaman* (published by Gollancz), an excellent account of his experiences as a wartime sailor. In his postscript he wrote something which will be true as long as there is a Navy.

> Seamen are not honoured because they get more for themselves than the rest of the messmates. They are not taught or forced to fight against each other. They learn to live in a community, sharing equally its terrors and its happiness, its miseries and its pleasures. They learn to help each other; and, in spite of everything that the sea may bring, the pull of this fellowship becomes increasingly strong.

64 HMS *Sabre*, a descendant of the coastal forces craft of the Second World War, but designed for training purposes

65 (*opposite*) HMS *Warspite*, a nuclear-powered fleet submarine which can go round the world without surfacing

Further Reading

Bernard Henry, *Vikings and Norsemen*, John Baker
Roger Hart, *The Battle of the Spanish Armada*, Wayland, Documentary History Series
John Hampden (ed.), *Hakluyt's Voyages*, OUP (documents about Elizabethan voyages)
John Hampden (ed.), *Seadogs and Pilgrim Fathers*, Ward, Golden Legends Series
The Voyages of Captain Cook, Jackdaw (a collection of facsimile documents and pictures)
Robert Southey, *Life of Nelson*, Dent, Everyman's Library
Roger Hart, *Nelson's Navy*, Wayland, Sentinel Books
Donald MacIntyre, *Trafalgar*, Lutterworth
C. S. Forester, The Hornblower novels: *Mr Midshipman Hornblower*; *A Ship of the Line*; *Flying Colours*; *Hornblower and the 'Hotspur'*; *Lord Hornblower*, etc.
Frederick Marryat, *Mr Midshipman Easy*, (various editions)
Frank Knight, *The Dardanelles Campaign*, Macdonald, Famous Events Series
N. Monsarrat, *The Cruel Sea*, Cassell, Cadet edition and others
S. E. Ellacott, *The Seamen*, (two volumes) Methuen. (Useful account of the life of the naval and merchant sailor through the ages)

Index

Aboukir Bay (Battle of the Nile), 52
Afrika Korps, 76
Albemarle, Duke of, 23, 35
El Alamein, 79
Alexandria, 75
American Independence, War of, 32, 40, 43
Anglo-Saxon seafarers, 7
Anson, Admiral Lord, 33, 38
Armada, Spanish, **7**, 13–16, 17
Artillery, 8
Assault ships, 89
Atlantic, Battle of, 78, 81
Atomic energy, 88
Ballads, 28, 29
Barracks, Royal Naval, 64
Beatty, Admiral Lord, 64, 65, 66
Britain, Battle of, 73
Blake, Robert, **11**, 23
Blane, Sir Gilbert, 39, 42
Bombs, 70
Boscawen, Admiral, 33, 35, 39, 40
Bounty payments, 43
Bowles, Admiral Sir William, 61
Bridport, Admiral Lord, 49
Burghley, Lord, 16, 17
Camperdown, Battle of, 47, 51
Cape Matapan, Battle of, 76
Cape St Vincent, Battle of, 46
Charles I, 19, 21, 23
Charles II, 23
Churchill, Winston, 35
Civil War, 19
Clothing, 17, **18, 19, 20**
Coastal Forces, **51**, 79, 82, 83, 84
Cockburn, Admiral Sir George, 60
Codrington, Admiral, 59
Collingwood, Admiral, 47, 55
Combined Operations, 79, 83
Commando ships, 89
Convoys, 67, 74, 78, 75, 80, 81
Cook, Captain James, 34, 38, 90
Copenhagen, Battle of, 52–53
Coral Sea, Battle of, 78
Coronel, Battle of, 65
Coronation Review of the Fleet, 86–87
Crete, 75, 76
Cromwell, Oliver, 20
Cunningham, Admiral, 76
Dakar, attack on French fleet, 75
Dardanelles expedition, **38**, 66
D-day, 83, 89
Desertion, 31, 32, 41, 43
Discipline, 17, 39
Disease, 36, 37, 38, 41, 42
Dogger Bank, Battle of, 65
Dover Patrol, 64
Drake, Sir Francis, 9, 10, 11, 12, 13, 15, 17, 8
Duncan, Admiral Lord, **26**, 51

Dunkirk evacuation, **46**, 72–73
Dutch Navy, **13**, 19, 23, 25
Dutch Wars, 20, 22, 25, 29
E-boats, 79
Edward III, 8
Elizabeth I, 9, 10, 19
English Succession, War of, 29
HMS *Excellent* (gunnery school), 47
Falkland Islands, Battle of, 65
Fishery protection, 90
Fisher, Admiral Lord, **37**, 64, 65
Fleet Air Arm, 74, 86
Food and drink, 15, 17, 21, 27, 30, 31, 38, 40, 51, 58, **60**, 62, 87
Fox, Charles James, 48
French Revolution, 43
Gallipoli, 66
Geddes Axe, 79
Glorious First of June, **24**, 46
Gunnery, 40, 61, 67
Harvey, Admiral Sir Edward, 61
Hawke, Admiral Lord, 33
Hawkins, Sir John, 9, 15
Heligoland, Battle of, 64
Henry VIII, 8
Hitler, Adolf, 69, 73–74
Hood, Admiral, **16**, 33
Howe, Admiral Lord, **24**, 43, 45, 46, 48, 49, 50
Howard of Effingham, Lord, 13
Hostels for sailors, 63
Hosier, Admiral Francis, 36
Hostilities Only sailors, 68, 86
Invergordon strike, 69
Iron ships, 60
James I, 19, 23
James II, 28
Java Sea, Battle of, 78
Jellicoe, Admiral Lord, **39**, 65, 66
Jervis, Admiral Sir John, 46, 47
Jutland, Battle of, **41**, 66, 67, 70
Keyes, Admiral Sir Roger, 67
Lagos, Battle of, 33
Lind, James, 38, 39
Lord Mayors' men, 45
Mallalieu, J. P. W., 92
Malta, 75, 76, 79, 80
Marine Society, 43
Marque, letters of, 19
Medical care, 16, 27, 58
Melville, Lord, 60
Mines, 61
Mountbatten, Admiral Lord, 88
Mussolini, Benito, 69
Mutiny, 17, 47, 48–51, 68
Napoleon, 47, 53, 54, 57, 58
Napoleonic Wars, 43–57

NATO exercises, 91
Naval conferences, 69
Navarino, Battle of, 59, 61
Navy Board, 20, 23
Nelson, Admiral Lord, **28**, **31**, 42, 45, 47, **51**, 52, 53, 54, 56, 61
Nile, Battle of the, 52
'New Albion', colony, 11
Nuclear weapons, 86
Paixhans, General, 61
Parker, Sir Hyde, 52, 53
Parker, Richard, 47, 51
Pay, 21, 22, 23, 31, **35**, 43, 48, 56, 60, 62
Pensions, 17, 27, 62
Pepys, Samuel, **12**, 25, 26, 27, 29, 30
Plate, Battle of River, **44**, 70–71
Polaris missiles, 88
Popham, Edward, 23
PQ17 (Russian convoy), 77–78
Press-gang, 18, **22**, 34, 38, 43, 58
Prize money, 17, 22, 27, 30, 33, 38
Promotion, 22, 62
Punishment, 18, 27, 39, 48, 59, 63
Purser, 17, **18**, 21, 27,
Quiberon Bay, battle of, **15**, 33, 40
Radar, 70, 82
Reuter, Admiral von, 68
Rodney, Admiral, 23, 39, 42
Rommel, Field-Marshal, 79
Russian convoys, 77, 78, 82
Saints, Battle of the, 33, 42
Saumarez, Admiral Sir James, 53
Scapa Flow, 64
Scurvy, 15, 38
Scuttling of German fleet, **43**, 68
Seven Years' War, 32, 38, 40
Ship money, 19
Ships:
   Achilles, 71, 90
   Ajax, 70, 71
   Ark Royal, **6**, **48**, 77
   Barham, 72
   Blenheim, **36**
   Campbeltown, 79
   Captain, 47, 51, 52
   Chesapeake, 59
   Courageous, 71
   Dreadnought, 64, 88
   Duke of York, 82
   Eagle, 80, 86
   Elizabeth, 10
   Excellent, 47
   Exeter, 70, 71
   Falkland, 30
   Formidable, 42
   Foudroyant, 45
   Fougeux, 56
   Gneisenau, 65, 70, 72
   Golden Hind, 10, 11, 15
   Golden Lion, 17
   Graf Spee, 70, 71
   Great Britain, 60
   Glorious, 72
   Hibiscus, **50**
   Hindenburg, **43**
   Illustrious, 75
   Inflexible, 65
   Invincible, 65
   Jamacia, 81
   Lion, 65
   London, 50
   Lützow, 71, 82
   Madre de Dios, 17
   Monarch, 49
   Namur, 35
   Nassau, 48
   Nautilus, 88
   Norfolk, **61**
   Phoebe, 90
   Prince of Wales, 77
   Queen Elizabeth, 77
   Redoubtable, **30**, 56
   Repulse, 77
   Resolution, 75
   Revenge, 55
   Rodney, 69
   Royal Charles, 25
   Royal Sovereign, **9**, 56
   Royal Oak, 27, 28, 71
   Sandwich, **25**, 51
   Santissima Trinidad, 47
   Shannon, 59
   Sheffield, 81
   Squirrel, 18
   Téméraire, 30
   Theseus, 51, 52
   Tirpitz, 77, 79, 82
   Valiant, 69, 77
   Vanguard, 52, 86
   Victory, **29**, **30**, **31**, 45, 54
   Ville de Paris, 42
   Vittorio Veneto, **47**
   Warrior, **34**, 61
   Warspite, 72
   Welshman, **52**, 80
Sicily, Allied invasion of, 81
Slave trade, 9, 59
Sluys, Battle of, 8
Spanish Main, 10
Spanish Succession, War of, 32
Steamships, 59–60
Submarines, **42**, 61, 64, 86, 88, 89; *see also* X-craft
Ticket, payment by, 23–24, 25, 31
Torpedoes, 61, 63, 70
Trafalgar, Battle of, 55, 56, 57, 59
Training, 62, 63
Tromp, Admiral, 20
U-boats, **53**, **54**, 67, 76, 77, 81, 82, 84
Uniform, 17, 62–63
United States Navy, 59, 67, 78
Vernon, Admiral, 33, 34, 35
X-craft, **59**, 82, 84